Tina is the mother of six amazing children and has been a tremendous inspiration to my wife and me in our parenting journey. *Cultivating the Souls of Parents* offers a comprehensive roadmap to the secret treasure buried in all of parenting: the opportunity for unparalleled personal growth and transformation.

Rev. Dean Nelson, National Outreach Director
Human Coalition Action

Tina's is a sage voice. Every time I've spent time with her, I have left wanting more of God. She's lived through the hills and the valleys with the Lord and is a gift to the body of Christ to, now, share what she's learned there with us!

Sara Hagerty, Author
Every Bitter Thing is Sweet and *Unseen: The Gift of Being Hidden in a World that Loves to be Noticed*

Tina Webb is a deeply spiritual, committed parent whose lens on faith and family challenges and inspires. All Christian parents need the kind of guidance, reassurance, and conviction she offers in *Cultivating the Souls of Parents.*

- **Mary Butler Coleman**, Executive Director
City of Promise

Cultivating the Souls of Parents is a blessing to read. Tina Webb writes with wisdom and grace every parent needs, speaking right to the heart with words of life and light. The call to cultivate our own hearts as parents so we can faithfully tend to our children is right on. Sixteen years in ministry to adolescents and their families brought me back to this truth again and again. Raising children is no quick trip around the block, but a long and challenging journey, and our children deserve our very best. Thanks to God, we can be immeasurably more, according to His power at work within us. Tina faithfully calls us back to the source of love, joy, peace, patience, kindness, goodness, gentleness, faithfulness and self-control so we can be all God desires for us to be. To God be the growth and the glory!

Keith Rogers, Life Groups and Growth Pastor
City Church

Cultivating the Souls *of Parents*

Cultivating the Souls *of Parents*

Facing Our Brokenness
Embracing His Likeness

by Tina Webb

Carpenter's Son Publishing

Published by Carpenter's Son Publishing, Franklin, Tennessee

Edited by Sherry Davis and Joanna Breault
Cover Design by Maria Webb and Tina Webb
Interior Layout Design by Tina Webb

ISBN: 978-1-952025-55-6

Printed in the United States of America

For more information visit tinawebb.net

Thanks to

Doug and our six children. I love you all dearly. Doug's co-workers at State Farm who wanted me to write this book. My extended family, friends, and prayer partners: Eileen, Kelley, Kendra, Tessa, Alayna, Lori, and Sena. I'm grateful for your faithful partnership and prayers. Also, Joan Hutter, for women's conferences that launch destiny. Mom and Julia Nelson, I'm grateful for your advice and encouragement. Special thanks to Sherry Davis and Joanna Breault for editing and encouraging me with this project. Long live editors! A special thanks to Jennifer Miskov for using your gifts and platform to help writers like me put Jesus first all the time and in everything. The Writing in the Glory Workshop was my launching pad of vision.

Thank you, God, my Creator and Breath of Life, I bow to you alone.

Table of Contents

From the Author

Families are the fabric from which society is constructed. Learning how to build a healthy family can take years. Inevitably, as parents, we face internal struggles caused by family stress, societal pressure, and even our own upbringing. Understanding the tender heart of our Heavenly Father goes a long way. He knows our brokenness and seeks to parent us as we parent our children. We learn as we grow in Him. We overcome personal and generational hurdles by the power of His Spirit, who is our counselor.

In this book, I share with you how God gently guided me through this journey – the healing, the pruning, and the courage needed to dig deep. He wants to do the same for you! Parenting is not only a process of learning how to love well; it is a journey of becoming an emotionally whole child of God.

He loves you, unconditionally!

Tina

Introduction

What a weird idea parenting is: one broken human being learning from another broken human being how to live life well. What value does God find in having imperfect adults struggle to raise children?

How do you think God views parenting? As a gentle Potter, I think He loves to observe the intricate chiseling away of our rough edges to reveal the power of redemption. Blessed redemption! The moment when our eyes are opened to our enslavement to sin and the sacrifice of our Savior! Jesus Christ is the door through which we become spiritually and emotionally whole. God knew us before we were in our mother's womb, and through every phase of life, even the season of raising kids, we can become what He had envisioned.

Perhaps as a church culture, we've focused too much on our goals, rather than God's intricate process. Our goal is to raise picture-perfect, well-behaved kids who grow up and get good jobs. Nothing wrong with this, right? However, let's consider the process and not the goal. The process—the journey of raising kids is difficult. Draining at times. Deeply personal. Parenting uncovers our immense need for God. A vibrant church community and regular bible study are essential parts of our faith journey. But they cannot take the place of those fruitful and somewhat supernatural encounters with the One who takes the broken pieces of our soul and turns them into a beautiful story.

Our goal-oriented American culture often focuses on the benefits of adulthood rather than the emotional requirements to handle adult life. We've heard the comment, "Kids grow up way too fast." It's true. Each generation races to grow up! We did, and our kids do. Cars, freedom, romance. Drinking, voting, and the like are our rewards for coming of age. Becoming an adult is like crashing through the finish line of a 400-meter dash. We celebrate it even though we are not emotionally mature enough to handle the rewards.

In our Western culture, after high school, we go off to college or find jobs, with usually no one except our like-minded peers to give us advice on how to think and how to live. Then we get married and become parents, or become single parents, who realize that in many ways, we are emotionally ill-equipped for the rigors of raising children.

At the front end of the parenting process, we do the best we know how. From sleep schedules to adolescent mood-swings, we scratch our heads to figure out the best way to help our kids. Our first tries often fail. Then we carry the weight of self-condemnation. Sometimes we feel emotionally defeated. No one ever told us that raising kids would uncover our own brokenness.

As we get older, the parenting process continues even after our children move out of the house and begin their own families. For many of us, that season of life becomes mostly helping our adult kids financially and babysitting the grandkids. Daily pressures shift from active parenting to the norms of aging and retirement. As we watch another generation grow up, sometimes we observe inherited behaviors that we had not seen before.

Doug and I have two sets of children. The first four were born pretty much every two and a half years of our marriage. The second set of children came when child #4 was ten. These two boys are about two years apart, so if you do the math, you discover that there are twenty years from our oldest to our youngest. Most people do not choose a twenty-year gap between groupings of kids. However, God's inspiration to have two more children has become one of the best experiences of surrender in my life. For whatever reason, God decided that our process of parenting young children and teens needed to continue into another generation. We are in our fifties now. Raising these two boys is similar to the life of parents who decide to adopt or foster young children when their birth children are older. What many parents like us find is that although family principles and identity are maintained—what we stand for and who we are—at times, our best intentions to train the youngest children are hindered. Parenting-fatigue is real. As Doug puts it, when you are an older parent, sometimes you need a divine boost to have the energy to raise a new generation of human beings.

I need to remind myself that this is a process where not only my kids but I, too, am learning how to live well and love well. I will never have a place where I can say as a parent, "I have arrived!" No, this process of parenting brings to light my emotional brokenness that God wants me to explore and bring to Him to remedy and make whole.

God wants to travel this road with us, not as a condemning voice but with whispers of gentle encouragement. He is for us, not against us. His affirmations strengthen us when we feel weak. He lifts our chins to look at Him, the Perfect Parent. As we keep our gaze fixed on Him, we gain His perspective on not only our children but also our journey from brokenness to wholeness.

Parenting can be if we let it, a process of brutally naked surrender to God who affirms our efforts and gives us courage on an adventure for which none of us are prepared.

Chapter One

†

The Bare and the Beautiful

God loves us despite the still. I'm still harsh. I'm still critical. I'm still anxious. For a recovering perfectionist, this is a big deal. God tapped me on my shoulder when I was a lost 16-year-old. One summer evening, Romans 5:8 came alive: 'While we were yet sinners, Christ died for us.' As a new Christian, I thought that redemption meant instant perfection—no more mistakes, missteps—wow, how wrong I was! Eternal fellowship with Him was secured, yes, but what I discovered and still discover is that on a practical level, I'm weak and far from perfect.

Aggravation. Discontentment. Pride. What words describe what you have been dealing with? I invite you to be brutally raw right now. This book is about facing our faults and letting Him love us to wholeness. Yes, God still loves us and desires us despite our imperfections and weaknesses. Do you believe that? Pause and think about your answer. We are "the Loved," "the Accepted," and "the Desired." Do any of those words surprise you? He may not like how we behave sometimes, but His acceptance is not based on our performance. He proved that on the Cross.

God invites us to Him in spite of our behavior and character flaws. He does not condemn us, but He guides us to a better way to live. Christlike. Virtuous. Virtue isn't a word that we often hear these days. A virtue is a quality that conforms to moral excellence. We all have virtues that need to be developed. One of mine is patience—with my kids as well as with myself. But God doesn't sit in heaven and watch me struggle to become more patient. He is present in my growth and your growth. He does not leave us to figure out how to become more Christlike by ourselves. He is our helper! Daily, He is our help in time of need. His mercies are new every morning. He's not looking for us to be spiritual all-stars; He is just asking for our honesty and vulnerability. He is safe. He forgives. He heals. He matures. You may have been a Christian for 30 years and still be tempted by embarrassing things or overcoming a bad temper or pride. God loves you despite the still.

He is not looking for us to be spiritual all-stars; He is just asking for our honesty and vulnerability.

The Deeper Work

The world has changed a lot in twenty years. My energy has a hard time keeping up with the pace of the times. Today's culture and focus on technology differ from what I remember as a kid. In some ways, Doug and I need divine fuel injection to stay on top of new social media apps, TV shows, and even American slang. Then is the age factor. Some of you get this because you waited until your late thirties to have kids. Whatever the reason, I'm not as quick to remain firm in the consequences that I've established for bad behavior as I was when I was in my twenties. It's pretty bad when my ten-year-old has to remind me of the consequence that I gave my eight-year-old the day before. Another couple we know has a similar family structure as ours—lots of kids spread over many years. They shared how their older kids say things like, "How come you let Peter get away with speaking to you like that? You wouldn't have put up with that when we were young!"

Raising kids involves a lot of energy. The work is more than potty training, teaching them how to do laundry, and being their chauffeur. These surface demands are what we usually focus on—the quick dinners, homework, or jerseys that need to be washed for the next day. But under the surface of parenting is a task many of us never prepare for: navigating the realm of the soul. Our souls. And our kids' souls. The immaterial part of us that houses our will, our thoughts, and our emotions. Parenting well requires a continuous examination of this mysterious part of our creation. We operate from it—heart motives, attitudes, triggers—but most of us don't know how to cultivate its ground.

But under the surface of parenting is a task many of us never prepare for: navigating the realm of the soul. Our souls. And our kids' souls.

The Soul – Issues of the Heart

It's not the daily routine that demonstrates the rigors of shepherding a young Mini-Me. That's easy compared to navigating heart motives and attitudes. Raising a child helps us discover that parenting involves a whole lot of digging, not just through piles of mismatched socks, but also through layers of insecurities and heart issues that our children and we have.

It takes courage and humility to look at a young child's behavior and realize that they are merely imitating us. What we say and how we say it. Ever been shocked to hear your little one say something with the same intonation that you would say it?

What about our actions? Our kids pick up so much! We cannot expect them to change if we are not willing to change also.

A great reward awaits the man or woman who decides to become a better person by tackling the unseen world of the soul. Letting Jesus renew our minds and mature our emotions is more effective than molding outward behavior through rules and "should." Rules serve a purpose but cannot replace the process of uprooting the seeds that cause behavior. When we take the time to listen to our words and think about our reactions, we can discover the source of the triggers, our attitudes, and our insecurities. God can also show us inherited behaviors that have not been unlearned or emotional wounds that have never closed.

Despite the surface-level rigors of raising kids, we can invite Him to help us do the work of uprooting these deep issues that keep us broken. Over time, we become adults who better reflect our God in word and deed. God uses every opportunity to smooth our rough edges and to lead us toward wholeness.

A man's pride will bring him low,
but the humble in spirit will retain honor.
Proverbs 29:23

Our Bare Reality

I had an anger issue. A scar sits on my right thumb, where I put my hand through a window. Years before this incident, when I was a junior in college, I was suicidal. The word "soul" wasn't in my vocabulary at that time, but mine was crying loudly for help. Anger and grief had brewed inside of me since I was five years old, but as a self-appointed "good" oldest child, I kept it at bay. I wore a mask. Unfortunately, anger quietly grew into self-loathing, self-rejection, and violence. I don't remember what led to my deciding to join a small group for anger issues. But after completing the workbook, doing weeks of homework, and getting prayer, I was free from pent-up childhood rage.

We are a society used to wearing masks. Many of us try to hide the ugliness within us. We carry shame and insecurities because we are not completely secure in the divine truth of what God thinks of us. We know Jesus died for us. But in our hearts, we wonder, *Is He mad at me?* After all, we knew better than to do *that* again, right? In church, we learn that He loves us without condition. But we ask ourselves, *Does He really accept me unconditionally?* Acceptance carries a different weight. It invites us to enter His holy presence even when we don't deserve to be there. In our uncertain state, we interact with Him at a comfortable distance. We maintain a surface-level relationship with Him. One built upon condition-based thinking: I can only ask Him for help if I fulfill a condition rather than knowing that we can freely enter His gracious presence any time we need Him (Heb 4:16). As we've been trained, we say grace at dinner, but then we ignore any family tension or lack of peace. We go to church and "put on" the acceptable Christian posture of stoicism, goodness, and of course, the smile. But shame and insecurity make us hide the deepest parts of ourselves from God and others.

We are a society used to wearing masks. Many of us try to hide the ugliness within us.

It takes courage to stop hiding. Without the mask, we would see ourselves in ways that we haven't wanted to. We are forced to acknowledge the areas that God still needs to purge. The act of removing our masks is a big decision. It means we are willing to bare ourselves to a world that can be so unforgiving.

But Jesus Christ forgives. Do you believe this? Do you live like you are forgiven? Smile like you are forgiven? With the weight of our sins removed, we should walk around like we know how loved we are! But most of us don't.

Acknowledging our weaknesses and mistakes takes great humility and an undeterred sense of self-worth. Think about this: you are worth the blood of God's Son. That's a big deal. When we realize our worth, our issues fall into their proper place. In other words, God's ability to transform will be magnified, not our mistakes. This perspective increases the ability for us to be honest with our kids about our weaknesses.

Self-evaluation is essential. What makes us slow to apologize to our children after raising our voice a little too loudly or not following up on a promise made? Do we fear being disrespected? Does apologizing make us feel weak? God wants to help us be comfortable looking our children in the eyes as the broken parts of ourselves become apparent. Our kids need to see our weaknesses. They need to know that we need God too. As far as the healthy soul searching that begins once the mask is off, the digging process is not for the faint of heart. Acknowledging our weaknesses and insecurities takes courage. But God gives us the courage we need.

For a healthy process to occur, self-condemnation must be packed away in a box marked with large red letters: Danger - Flammable. We are who we are and where we are at this point in our life's journey. We have to accept it without taking on shame. At the beginning of this journey towards wholeness, you may ask yourself these questions: "How can I train and raise children when I'm so broken? What will my teenagers say when I get a better understanding of God and His authority in our lives and then adjust our lifestyle to that reality? Now that I've put aside my mask to acknowledge my brokenness, will my kids or my spouse accept me?"

These questions are legitimate. As we heal and mature, we will become more comfortable with our parental authority. Our kids will notice. They may not like it because our wholeness will affect how we train them. They may balk at an increase in house rules or smartphone boundaries. We must resist getting angry at their reactions. After all, we must take responsibility for what we have or have not modeled. They will need time to adjust to transitions. During these moments of chaos and tension, the best escape for us is in prayer. In fact, prayer time is crucial in this process. I'm speaking of prayer as honest, vulnerable, hold-nothing-back conversation with God. Like what David did in many of his Psalms. Ask Him for strength. Pray for the courage to continue moving forward in growth even when it's hard. Prayer is vital to soul healing. During those moments, we can vent to the One who is not offended by our emotions.

During those moments, we can vent to the One who is not offended by our emotions.

He who knit us in our mother's wombs will continue to make the fabric of our families something beautiful. It will take time. There will be tears and fights. As you share with your spouse or children about your new journey, the highs of self-discovery, and the lows of hard choices, your words will be seeds that will make an impression in the long run.

When we begin to tackle our broken humanity, God often uses us to repair unhealthy places in our extended family system. Sometimes, God uses us as He did Moses – to show our extended family the way out of generational bondage. The road seems daunting, but God is faithful.

"He who began a good work in you will perfect it
until the day of Christ Jesus."
Philippians 1:6

Failed but Not a Failure

Eli was a priest. How in the world did the sons of a priest become corrupt? Not only did they did not know the sacrificial customs, but they also committed fornication. It was their dad's fault. According to 1 Samuel 3:13, God saw that "he did not restrain them."

Now the sons of Eli were corrupt;
they did not know the LORD.
1 Samuel 2:12

… his sons made themselves vile, and ***he did not restrain them.***
1 Samuel 3:13

It sounds like Eli could have stopped his sons from going down a dark path, but he didn't. Eli did not teach them to honor the system of offerings and sacrifices, and he greedily took the best of what the people brought for their offerings. The verse speaks of "the iniquity which he knows." Iniquity is the biblical term for inherited weakness or inherited sin. This makes me think that Eli failed to train his sons on how to resist bad family patterns of behavior. Perhaps when his sons were mischievous boys, he did not discipline them. Maybe he catered to their whining and excuses and never helped them see the sin in their hearts through gentle and honest conversation. In verse 27, God speaks to Eli through a prophet; and later He speaks through a young boy named Samuel. (1 Sam 3:13) Through these prophetic voices, Eli faced the harsh reality of his failed parenting style and the resulting consequences to his lineage. When we see him finally warning his sons in 1 Samuel 2:22, it's too late. He is old, and they are grown men. As a priest, what would have caused Eli to fail to train his sons?

In this story, we learn that Eli did not revere God enough, did not respect the system of repentance that God set up, hadn't acknowledged his issues, and was eventually confronted with the scandal of his sons. Propitiation for their sinful behavior was available through the Hebrew custom of blood sacrifice, but the sons scoffed at the customs. When Eli tried to reason with them, it was too late. Now grown men, they were unrepentant, promiscuous, and defiant. Eli missed the opportunity to guide and train them during their formative years.

Now Eli was very old, and he heard everything his sons did to all Israel, and how they lay with the women who assembled at the door of the tabernacle of meeting. So he said to them, "Why do you do such things? For I hear of your evil dealings from all the people. No, my sons! For it is not a good report that I hear. You make the LORD's people transgress."
1 Samuel 2: 22-24

Eli wasn't a total screw-up. Despite his paternal negligence, God allowed him to mentor the young Samuel, who was called from an early age to be a prophet. In fact, God revealed the consequences of Eli's sin to the boy Samuel, in a vision. Samuel witnessed firsthand not only the humiliation of his mentor but his submission to the fate of his family.

When we are confronted with our issues, we have the opportunity to embrace change. It's our choice. Change takes humility, courage, and grace. Eli lived under the Old Testament covenant and did not have the benefit of God's grace like we do.

What is grace? It's undeserved favor. We don't deserve God's favor, but the decision to give our lives to Christ qualifies us. Grace can also be described as the divine strength and ability that He extends to us for change to occur. Miraculously, when we became born again, when we chose Him, we took part in a covenant. Jesus exchanged our sinfulness for His righteousness. We didn't have to earn it. We just received His gift. The gift of Christ brought spiritual redemption. Our spirits are realigned with God. But our souls need to receive His enabling grace.

We are spirit, soul, and physical body. Being born again, or "born of the Spirit" (John 3:3-17), initiates the process of becoming whole. This is the beginning. As far as our souls, our minds still need renewing (Rom. 12:1), our emotions need repairing (3 John), and the human will must yield. This journey involves letting God do unseen and somewhat mysterious changes in the depths of our souls.

Free from Guilt

Not everything that your child does wrong is your fault. As adults, we are imperfect human beings raising other imperfect human beings. Our kids also have souls (mind, will, and emotions) that need to be aligned with God's intent and design. Our behavior is not all bad, and it's not all good. His blood has removed our sinful nature, but we must unpack hidden emotional issues that still cause us to stumble. Sometimes we assume that when we sin, it is an act of the will. We can just stop. However, there are underlying reasons why sometimes we cannot just stop. God wants to uncover these hindrances. They can be inherited negative propensities or unresolved hurts. While following rules and maintaining boundaries protect us from unnecessary failures and reading parenting books gives us wisdom, they cannot wholly align our souls to God's intent. Only He can do that.

His blood has removed our sinful nature, but we must unpack hidden emotional issues that still cause us to stumble.

We are fallible parents who still need guidance and help. Our journey from brokenness to wholeness will be easier if we internalize this truth: we are treasured, and we are desired by a perfect God! In Christ, we are forgiven! Our worth cannot be based on how well we do, but on the fact that our very existence is significant to God.

The Old Testament did not offer the option for redemption, but the New Testament does through the blood sacrifice, resurrection, and ascension of Jesus Christ. This initiating heart of God is a relief for today's parents who may have been "Eli's" at one time and whose adult children are now prodigals. It is possible for these adult children, whose hearts and minds are far from God's best, to be wooed by the Spirit of God. The course of a lineage can be altered by the grace of God through Jesus Christ.

Grace to Change

I believe in a Creator who imagined each of us out of the goodness of His nature. Sin came, but God's grace continuously releases the power to be transformed. We must keep our eyes on the process—the change that occurs while we raise our kids. As we begin to examine parts of our souls, we will realize the benefit of having God's favor and merit when we don't deserve it. Grace, God's lovingkindness, truly transforms the human heart. Here are a few scriptures that we can ponder.

Cause me to hear Your lovingkindness…
Cause me to know the way in which I should walk,
For I lift up my soul to You.
Psalm 143:8

Who redeems your life from destruction, who crowns you
with lovingkindness and tender mercies
Psalm 103:4

Or do you think lightly of the riches of His kindness
and tolerance and patience, not knowing that the kindness of
God leads you to repentance?
Romans 2:4

Romans 2:4 is an overwhelming truth! Repentance means a change of mind. When are mindsets change, our behavior will follow. This scripture reminds us to treasure and to appreciate His patience and goodness even when we fail miserably. This continual kindness on His part affects our hearts and wills in a way that promotes change. The Bible also teaches that when we recognize our failings and our weaknesses and bring them into the light, not suppressing, ignoring, or denying them, we will receive grace to help in our times of need (Hebrews 4:16).

Similarly, when we recognize that we are not "sufficiently qualified in ourselves to claim anything as coming from us, but our sufficiency and qualifications come from God" (2 Cor. 3:5 AMP), we can choose to believe in and forever submit to God who creates us and therefore can change us. All is not lost! The beauty of God's grace is that we can bring our embarrassing shortcomings to God who is waiting to forgive and mend.

If you are married, picture God between you and your spouse. He is your connecting point. Now picture Him in between but elevated above your heads. He is your good heavenly Daddy waiting to mentor you. He wants to be known by your kids and will do whatever necessary to guide their hearts toward Him. If you are a single parent or a guardian, your picture is similar. I envision our heavenly Daddy behind you, with His arms wrapped around you to comfort you. You can lean on Him. Like an orchestra conductor training His apprentice, He has each of His hands on your forearms. He'll help you direct the children He's blessed you with.

He Teaches Us All Things

One of my sons was a precious, bald one-year-old with a great throwing arm. His aim was uncanny. So, when a glass-topped end table was broken from a block that he threw as he stood at the top of the family room staircase, I decided that I needed to baby proof the house of all glass. Unfortunately, manufacturers don't make plastic windows.

Our quandary was how to make this little human realize that throwing a foam baseball to Daddy in the family room was okay, but throwing a wooden block towards glass in the house was not. My son saw the broken glass tabletop and noted the chagrin on my face. At the time, I wasn't sure if my facial expression was enough to give him pause before he threw something again. I found out that it was not. We realized for the next few years that this son continuously needed to be reminded of how to weigh consequences before playing with certain toys. Arrows are meant to be shot at targets, not over houses. After attempting to shoot an arrow over our house with his bow, this son implanted it in the roof. We had to borrow a tall ladder. You can be sure that Doug did not enjoy climbing up onto the roof to retrieve the arrow. "Think before you act, son." Situations like this helped me learn to seek the Holy Spirit's help when I was trying to figure out how to communicate lessons to each child. They also taught me to keep calm when kids do childish things.

Because as parents, we are so busy, it often takes us a while to sense the prompting of the Lord. His warnings. His hints. Those subtle suggestions that come to mind, but we dismiss too quickly because we are so fastened to our schedules and our opinions. But the Holy Spirit is always trying to communicate to us how to raise each child. Each one has specific gifts. Personalities. Needs. When one of our kids was in elementary school, God uncovered an emotional need that he had.

Often, it takes us awhile to sense the prompting of the Lord. His warnings. His hints.

During these years, we didn't let our kids watch certain PG-13 or any R movies. But at seven, one had a huge need to feel like he belonged. I hadn't picked up on this and got angry when he repeatedly asked to watch a movie that his peers had watched. This went on for weeks. Finally, one afternoon when he asked again, I inwardly criticized the other parents.

Unfortunately, in my state of criticism, I failed to perceive my son's valid longing. He wanted to feel like he belonged. That afternoon, the Lord was able to penetrate my bad attitude and my blindness. I went to my bedroom to let God do some heart surgery. "Lord, I messed up. I'm sorry." I thanked Him for the gift of forgiveness. Then I perceived His wisdom for the situation. What my husband and I allowed or disallowed didn't have to change, but the way I explained these things to our broken and hurting child needed to change. God had been trying to teach me how to pastor my son's perception of not belonging. He wanted me to help my son unravel why he felt like an outsider. Was it just the one movie, or was it something deeper? That day I prayed, "God, help me tend to my son's hopes and needs, yet explain to him why we can't do something just because others do it. Help his need to belong not to be tied to the actions of others. Heal any wound of rejection that is deep in his soul. Give me the words that he'll understand so that he can be at peace with our decision to not see this one movie yet. Forgive me for leaning to my understanding, letting my opinions blind me to his brokenness, and not slowing down enough to pay attention to Your still, small voice."

I went to my bedroom to let God do some heart surgery. "Lord, I messed up. I'm sorry."

Finally, I had the right conversation with my son. I explained that we will always be friends with people who think differently and have a different family lifestyle. But, those differences cannot determine our course. As we talked, my son learned that God helps each family navigate through life to become a beautiful representation of His Son. We should never criticize another family's journey. We are all being guided by a good and holy God.

And why do you look at the speck in your brother's eye, but do not consider the plank in your own eye? Or how can you say to your brother, 'Let me remove the speck from your eye,' and look, a plank is in your own eye? Hypocrite! First remove the plank from your own eye, and then you will see clearly to remove the speck from your brother's eye.
Matthew 7:3-5

As Christian parents, we will discover the biblical truths that trump societal norms and cultural traditions. Society and culture are too unstable to provide a rock-solid foundation for Jesus-focused families. For example, God's purpose for humanity, first mentioned in Genesis 1:28, has never changed. Even sin's entrance in Genesis 3 didn't change God's original intent. A man and a woman are called to join in a covenant relationship, to steward this realm, and to produce offspring that do the same. This stewardship call is individual because like the Apostle Paul, not everyone will marry. The call is also for each generation. God is a generational God and producing offspring is a key reason for marriage. By the way, if you are an unmarried parent, your singleness doesn't disqualify you! Using these truths as our platform, we discover how God wants to design our individual families. We can teach our children that Israel had twelve sons, and each son's tribe had their distinctions, but all were His covenant people.

As Christian parents, we will discover the biblical truths that trump societal norms and cultural traditions.

My son was still disappointed and for months, he continued to bring up the "Why can't we watch this movie" type of questions. I had to stifle my frustration that he "just isn't getting it." God had to give me a perspective to cultivate patience in my life. He reminded me that my role is to train and that these conversations would continue as long as they were needed. God didn't mind them, and I shouldn't either. Training takes years.

There are endless opportunities for us to allow God to show us the soul issues that not only hinder our maturity but also hinder our effectiveness as parents. A wrong mindset is one. A critical attitude is another. As we become self-aware, we can spend time in prayer and reflection and allow Him to direct our way toward change. He wants to help us notice those inner promptings and discern His still, small voice. With every child and situation, He teaches us to pause and seek His direction.

Our Life, Our Story

From wandering wilderness seasons to gratifying mountain peak moments, we experience times of defeat and victory. Our Adolescent Story may have chapters of disappointment. Our Young Adult Story might have looked like a meandering river. Becoming a person of faith is undoubtedly the epiphany of Our Life Story. We hope and pray that this gut-wrenching, nail-biting drama called Life ends well for all involved. In terms of parenting, no matter how many books we read, friends we meet for coffee, or how much babysitting we did as teens, we are never adequately advised and prepared for the drama that unfolds once that first child comes into our home. The blessed Parent Story! What a surprise when we feel the love overflow as we gaze, cuddle our helpless newborn, or feel the hand clutch from a newly adopted child! Our hearts incessantly burn with an inexplicable love for our kids. Children are wonderful. We can give them wonder-filled lives. Sure, our best efforts are sometimes

Our Adolescent Story may have chapters of disappointment. Our Young Adult Story might have looked like a meandering river.

ineffectual. However, we keep trying. Yes, sometimes, in our responses and reactions, we don't love well. Our humanity will look uglier than we ever knew it could be. Allowing ourselves to be changed by this journey is worth it. Like the scripture says, our latter will be better than our past. (Revelation 21: 4)

Let's embrace the rigors of personal transformation and be grateful that our little mirrors make us self-aware. I encourage you to refrain from guilt and self-condemnation. God is One that comforts and encourages. (1 Thessalonians 5:11). He is a loving guide, not a harsh dictator. We can rest in His goodness and allow our years of raising kids to serve as opportunities to be molded by the hand of our loving Creator.

Time to Plant a Fruit Tree

But the fruit of the Spirit is love, joy, peace, patience, kindness, goodness, faithfulness, gentleness, self-control, against such there is no law.

Galatians 5:22-23

Galatians 5:22-23 calls these virtues the "fruit of the Spirit." Fruit comes from seeds. And so do weeds. Our souls: heart motives, attitudes, and triggers, will reveal the hindrances—the weeds—that that God wants to remove. But how do we dig deep to discover negative seeds? How do we uproot these hindering root systems? One way is to analyze our self-talk. If I continually badger myself when I don't do well, more than likely, a seed of perfectionism or self-condemnation was sown at some point. When I badger my children, I see what that seed has produced.

This scripture gives us a simple assessment that we can follow. Periodically, ask yourself: "How is my patience meter?" or "How often do my children see me joyful?" If our answers are not what we want them to be, let's not beat ourselves up. Instead, let's understand the process of developing good fruit. If our fruit of self-control is small or unripe, then we can look down into our souls or back into our pasts and discover why. Perhaps we have buried anger that comes out in conflict and causes us to say things that we later regret. Or maybe as children, our families didn't make much money, so as adults, we subconsciously spend more money than we ought because we finally have substantial financial resources.

How often do my kids see me joyful?

This plant analogy also addresses the good fruit in our lives. Any gardener knows that to produce continued growth, you have to prune a plant from time to time. Our Creator helps us by gently pruning us. As we allow His supernatural presence to invade our lives and cultivate the soil of our souls, and as we meditate on Scripture, the fruit of the Spirit will prosper.

This journey is a long adventure. It strips us bare. No more pride. Masks removed. We say yes to being vulnerable and transparent with God and others. But God does not give us more than we can bear. He works in increments—seasons where sometimes we dig up root issues, and other times we experience the fruitfulness of His work in us. He cleans us up and makes us beautiful. He turns our history into a mighty testimony. Our future becomes better than our pasts. For us and for our kids. God's vision is for generations of self-aware, autonomous adults who are not only responsible but are also emotionally healthy.

Prayer

God, thank you for loving me. Thanks for drawing me to the Cross and taking my sins upon Yourself. You want me to have abundant life—vitality in my spiritual, emotional, mental, and physical well-being. This is your desire for my kids and me. Some of my weaknesses are apparent. Others, I try to hide. You said in 1 Corinthians 5:17 that I am a new creation, but often, I don't feel changed. Where is the fruit of the Spirit in my life? Lord, there are days where I face the consequences of a sin, reminders of my imperfections, and feelings of regret that I haven't laid at the Cross…when am I going to feel like an overcomer?

Holy Spirit, I need You to bring a constant flow of Christ's transformative power into my life. Help me meditate on the fact that You don't condemn me. You encourage me. Thanks for being my Wonderful Counselor.

Quiet Time

Is there a section of this chapter that stands out to you? Take notes or reflect on the parts that resonated with you.

What is your self-talk like? Counter any condemning thoughts with scripture verses declaring who you are in Christ.

Ask the Lord to reveal any soul issue (an insecurity, inherited dispositions, an attitude, mentality, or emotional longing) that He wants to heal or refine. Think about where the issue may have come from.

Chapter Two

†

Road to the Spirit Life

The Bible is clear that faith involves taking hold of God's supernatural help in our lives. God desires to teach us to trust in what we cannot see and sometimes cannot understand. The Bible says that God displaced Jacob's hip to cause him to lean on Him for the rest of his life. But what does "leaning" look like in our daily lives?

One morning after dropping off my kids at school, I had a meeting with a fellow mom about ideas for our school's parent association. We reached the close of our conversation and began to pack up. Then I paused. I had a sense that I should slow down my pace of packing up. Somehow, I knew that there was something to come. Four minutes later, we both stared at each other in amazement. We realized that what we thought was our closing conversation had delved into a spiritual topic, one that we knew was divinely ordained. We stayed seated. It wasn't time to leave yet because God had mysteriously caused us to meander in a conversation that He wanted us to have. Without knowing it, she confirmed an idea that I had just given to Doug two days before. Similarly, when I shared my interest in God's desire to redeem family lines, I hit a bullseye in an area that she'd been giving some thought. We both laughingly commented that we were elated to find someone else who thinks about these topics.

God set us up! Or He had a purpose for our meeting that we didn't realize. Our conversation paved the way to personal God confirmations because we recognized and yielded to a "holy delay." This is part of leaning on God as He guides us to a destination that we can't see. It is the Spirit-led road. We don't always understand it, but it's for our benefit. Becoming a Spirit-led person helps us navigate parenting issues that challenge us due to our inexperience.

This is part of leaning on God as He guides us to a destination that we can't see.

One of my biggest hindrances in staying on this Spirit-led road is the issue of control. Years ago, I heard the phrase, "Let go, and let God." It's a good reminder to trust Him. Regularly, I pray that I will "lean not to my own understanding" (Proverbs 3:5-6), and "commit my works (plans) to the Lord so that my thoughts will be established" (Proverbs 16:3). The road involves yielding. Slowing down enough to catch His hints. Can we keep one ear on our child who is ranting and the other ear on Him, who can reveal to us any soul wound behind the rant? Did someone hurt her feelings at school? Is she frustrated over a bad grade? He will help us discern what is going on.

When it comes to our personal goals, we can trust that He will help us complete them in His timing. If we don't trust Him, we will be frustrated when our goals are blocked. Many underlying reasons keep us from trusting Him. Doubting His love for us, pride, disappointment from an unanswered prayer are some examples. Discovering these hindrances and letting Him tend to our souls, will bring the closure we need to let God have control of every aspect of our lives. He wants to help us embrace spontaneity and learn to hold personal dreams and daily plans with an open hand. We can remind ourselves that God's ways are better than anything that we could dream or plan.

The mind of man plans his way,
but the Lord directs His steps.
Proverbs 16:9

Leaning Means Trusting

I homeschooled for twenty years with no plans to stop. But in January of 2016, God repeatedly let me know that He had ordained a remarkable life change for our family. I loved being a home educator. Like any job, it had moments of challenge and frustration. But I really enjoyed the process of teaching my kids, observing the "aha" moments, and spending time with them. But I knew when we decided to have two more children that God had something different planned for them. I just didn't know what or why.

I grieved the change. Although I was excited to explore pursuits that I'd set aside, I spent the first week of school in a state of shock. I leaned on Him heavily in my sadness. No more snuggles on the couch before starting schoolwork. Instead, our mornings became a frenzied race to leave the house on time.

My life belonged to God. These were His children that I was charged to steward. If homeschooling was no longer in His plan for them, then I had to trust and follow His lead.

This Spirit-life not only requires forsaking control, but it requires an understanding that we are conditioned to obtain everything by our own effort. America teaches that we must pull ourselves up by our own bootstraps. But rugged individualism and self-sufficiency is a paradigm that leaves God out of the equation. God gets the most glory when we realize that we have to let Him take the lead in every aspect of our lives.

Trust in the Lord completely,
and do not rely on your own opinions.
With all your heart rely on him to guide you,
and he will lead you in every decision you make.
Become intimate with him in whatever you do,
and he will lead you wherever you go.
Don't think for a moment that you know it all,
for wisdom comes when you adore him with undivided devotion.
Proverbs 3:5-7a, The Passion Translation

The Spirit of Wisdom

As a young mother, the voices of other women sharing their parenting styles, house cleaning schedule, and weekly devotional routine would echo in my head. After my second child was born, and I became a stay-at-home mom, I worked hard to be like them! I wanted to be viewed as successful. Their lives seemed to mirror God's wisdom. So I pushed myself, even when was carrying another child, and up at night consoling a sick toddler. My life was a pressure cooker, and I didn't turn the power button off until many years later.

Wisdom comes with age; that is no lie. Looking back, I wasted so much internal energy operating out of a desire for approval instead of trusting the Holy Spirit to design my family life in the way that worked best for us.

Sometimes when we are learning what it means to "hear the voice of God," a phrase used in some Christian churches, we become disillusioned because it seems so hard. Later we realize that God isn't talking to us audibly. His still, small voice can come in the form of a "holy delay" or an unexplainable hesitation. He speaks to us through Scripture, through our dreams, and when we pray and worship. In our parenting, we learn how to move from a self-effort life to Spirit life through practice.

Ephesians 1:17-20 presents secrets that many Christians miss as they journey throughout life. Understanding 1) God's intents and 2) the power believers have access to, has helped me parent differently now than I did twenty years ago.

...that the God of our Lord Jesus Christ, the Father of glory, may give to you the spirit of wisdom and revelation in the knowledge of Him, the eyes of your understanding being enlightened; that you may know what is the hope of His calling, what are the riches of the glory of His inheritance in the saints, and what is the exceeding greatness of His power toward us who believe, according to the working of His mighty power which He worked in Christ...
Ephesians 1:17-20

Our God is a relational being who embodies beneficence and perfect love. Scripture reading gave me a mental understanding of this, but my life journey instilled the truth into my heart. Experiencing God's faithfulness year after year and tuning my heart to His affirming whispers helped me know—become intimately acquainted with—Him. He loves me. He desires me. He stays with me. Once I realized that I was already accepted by Him, that I could not do anything to prove that I was worth saving and that I could not do anything to remove His love from me so many insecurities faded away.

Likewise, when I took time to really think through the many Scriptures that say that the Spirit of God dwells in me, I realized that I could "tap into" His ability and power in a way that would make the daily cross of struggle so much lighter. He could empower me with divine wisdom for each child and each situation. It changed how I lived and how I raised our kids.

Along with His wisdom comes His mighty power. Sometimes our kids and we face challenges that seem impossible to overcome. Sometimes human ability falls short. Scripture teaches us that nothing is impossible for God (Luke 1:37). He wants this truth to be more than a mental understanding. When we pray, we can ask for His power to be released into situations (1 Corinthians 2:5). We can ask for Him to remove habits and inherited predispositions like perfectionism, fear, or control from our lives. The mighty power that came down from Heaven to resurrect Jesus' dead body is hard to imagine. It's the same power that transported Jesus from the earthly realm into Heaven. To think that God wants to empower us as His vessels is an important realization. It gives us confidence that He is determined to help us throughout our day.

We can ask for His power to be released in situations.

This power is one thing that causes our lives as believers to be different than that of nonbelievers. The ability of God to work in and through my life as a parent gives me hope and vision for my children's divine destiny. As I began to believe the fact that His angels were in my vicinity every day, waiting to help me and that His presence was just a pause away, it changed how I was as a person and, therefore, as a parent. "Help me, Lord" became a frequent phrase throughout my day. And He did!

Letting Go of Self-Sufficiency

Allowing His presence and power to permeate every conversation and every attitude that I had with my children meant yielding my perfection-laden mindset to Him. Self-effort had to go. I can't make myself a better mom, but I could open my heart to the One who can. I needed to trust God to do what I could not do by myself. When I was weak, He wanted to reveal to me that He had strength to give me—a supernatural dose of mental fortitude or emotional endurance. When I was exhausted and hopeless, He brought comfort through other moms who, like me, realized that when our masks came off—once perfectionism and fear of disapproval were removed, true comfort and mutual ministry could happen. We learned to be "real" and vulnerable about our needs.

In the mid-1990s, Doug and I had temporary custody of a niece and nephew. Every day I had six children under the age of seven to mother. My most vivid memory is a woman at our church who came over to our small apartment and just dealt with the massive pile of unpaired socks, with toys and toddlers just feet away. Another favorite memory is a friend, who also had children the same age, who left her kids at home to tend to mine when I was sick in bed with the flu. Those precious few hours saved my emotional state when I was physically undone.

God never wants the enemy of our lives to have a victory. He'll take the worst experience and over time, make it a valuable testimony.

God causes all things bad that happen to be reworked in order to bring out good. God never wants the enemy of our lives to have a victory. He'll take the worst experience and over time, make it a valuable testimony. Life was hard back then, but it became a good part of my story, a chapter in which I learned how He seeks to help me and guide me at every turn.

Meeting my practical needs was important, but more important was the way God changed me from the inside out. The soul work. I asked the Holy Spirit to show me where my mind needed to be renewed (Romans 12:1). I had to let go of fears of making mistakes with my kids, of not keeping a tidy house or having kids who weren't trained in good manners. So what if the house stays messy for an entire weekend? Hear me, I didn't let go of the knowledge that these things are good. I let go of the fears that put me in bondage to these things. There is quite a difference.

Where to Begin

At first, it can seem hard to make time to spend with God. Morning quiet times don't work for everyone, but the Holy Spirit is available any time of day! The Israelites prayed at appointed times throughout the day. God will show you where and how to rearrange your schedule. Just ask Him. When I was pregnant with my third child, I began to set aside a personal quiet time every day. I managed to get my four-year-old to play quietly for two hours while the two-year-old napped. During this time, I kneeled on my floor and prayed. Often, I dozed off—raising small kids is exhausting! However, my Bible would be in front of me open, and when I woke up, I would glance at another scripture to meditate on or pray through. Christian worship music would play in the background so that if I was too tired to ponder Scripture, I could focus on the words of a particular song. God met me during these times. I learned the beautiful work of intercession as I began to pray for the life of my unborn baby or Doug, who was working eighty hours per week. Looking back at this special time in my life, I know the Holy Spirit healed many wounds and erased many scars while I kneeled in His presence. I know He planted the seeds of future dreams into my heart. Most of all, He convinced me during these quiet moments that He was for me and would always be my help.

I know the Holy Spirit healed many wounds and erased many scars while I kneeled in His presence.

Bringing Him glory is achieved not through self-effort but by yielding to the unseen movement of His Spirit in us and around us. The life He wants for us involves a path that we can't determine ahead of time. We have to practice listening to His still, small voice and pausing when we sense a "holy delay." His Spirit provides wisdom for every situation. As we surrender our fears, He matures us and designs a better life for our families than we could imagine.

Prayer

Father, You know the plans that You have for my family and me. They are good. Your promises are sure. Honestly, God, sometimes I forget to rely on You. Sometimes I go about my days and don't invite You into every moment and every conversation. Please forgive me. Rework my life, my thinking, and our family schedule to give us time to spend with You—time to build our relationships with You in the beauty of quiet reflection. Help us be aware of Your still, soft voice that directs our steps. Lord, I want to be available for others! I want to submit to "holy delays" when You are bringing about something for a reason. Keep me from leaning to my own understanding and reasonings. Help me embrace a Spirit-life where I am led by You in ways that will defy my logic and reasoning. Wow me, Lord! Your ways are better than mine. Your understanding will always be higher than my own!

Quiet Time

What do you think about your relationship with God?

What do you think God thinks about you?

Does any aspect of your parenting reflect your previous answers?

Chapter Three

†

Holy Restriction vs. Legalism

So many of us have been harmed by well-intentioned pastors and Christian teachers. They, too, are in a process; however, we don't usually give them the grace to grow and deal with their own brokenness. Some of us have become bitter towards those who made recommendations to change behavior but didn't address the unseen soul issues that contributed to the behavior. In the eyes of many believers, these well-meaning recommendations reveal legalism. Religious legalism, in my experience, is a generational, cultural, or denominational propensity toward promoting restrictions that seem right but are based on fear and unawareness. Pastors of various backgrounds can be afraid of congregants "falling into sin," and the "falling" spreading like a contagion. Or they may be fearful that God's name will be dishonored. However, this fear isn't pronounced. It's hidden, as many of our root issues are. Fear can often be disguised as wisdom. I address this later in the book. Like you and me, many Christian leaders are unaware of how to address their own brokenness. Not only that but addressing soul wounds and insecurities takes them time and space. Time to reflect and the space to be who they are, not who we want them to be. Too often, we put leaders on an unfair pedestal and expect perfection. But all of us carry unhealthy inherited weaknesses and emotional hurt.

There is a fine line between legalism and wise restriction. For example, as parents, when we know that our kids may stumble into something we view as immoral, we put up restrictions. These can be parental controls on a computer or not allowing them to go out with a member of the opposite sex alone. Those restrictions are wise, promoting safety for young people whose decision-making functions are not fully developed. However, we need to monitor our hearts and make sure that we don't accidentally impart a fear of failure or a sense of *conditional* acceptance. We don't want our kids to be afraid of making a mistake. We want them to come to us when they fail, not hide from us. That's what God wants from all of us when we fail. All of us. Leaders. Parents. Singles. Kids. As believers, we have His unconditional love and acceptance. No matter what. His love and acceptance are based on our faith in Jesus Christ and the blood He shed, not our works.

We want them to come to us when they fail, not hide from us.

To avoid misrepresenting the Father's heart, we can make sure that our kids understand that a specific restriction may not be biblically based, for example, not being alone with the opposite sex when there is mutual attraction. Restrictions can be flexible and based on their age and stage of emotional development. Legalism is usually rigid. It raises its ugly head when it puts a cultural or parental limit on par with the Word of God.

Being tempted is not sinful. Jesus Christ was tempted in all points. Consider that. Have you felt guilty for being tempted? Jesus was tempted by every sin in existence and bore no guilt because guilt is a consequence of sin. He never sinned. When it comes to temptation, we can ask God to show us what in our soul makes a particular thing tempting. There could be a seed thought that was planted in our minds as kids. Perhaps one of our parents had this temptation as well. Our emotional wiring—our predispositions, can be genetic. Let's not get scared when we are tempted, or we find that our kids caved to temptation. We want to avoid parenting in and from fear. We can just ask God to help us dig and find the answers. This is the loving route. This verse from James is a great one to dissect as we try to create a healthy environment that will nourish our children, one that is not fear-based.

But each one is tempted when he is carried away and enticed by his own lust.
James 1:14 (NKJV)

To discover what makes us lean to a particular lust, we need to first define lust. This Greek word, *epithumia,* means a strong desire. Some New Testament passages use this word to convey a strong desire that is good. Others place the word in the context of evil desires. This particular verse indicates being drawn away and enticed which implies strong desires that are contrary to God's design and intent for us. The wording in this translation reveals 1) a strong personal desire or one that we "own," and 2) this desire has the *power* to draw us away from what we know is best. It has the power to seduce. But why?

Asking the question, "Why am I tempted by this?" can lead to discovering the strong desires in the seedbed of our souls. When we ask ourselves, what makes us be pulled by something, whether it's attention or immoral thoughts, we begin the digging process. This process should not begin without first asking the Holy Spirit to lead and guide us in the way that we should go. He will steer us because He knows what is there. During this process, we may journal or just sit quietly and let Him guide our thoughts. Pretty much every morning I pray Psalm 19:14. *Let the words of my mouth and the meditation of my heart be acceptable in Your sight,*

O Lord, my rock and my Redeemer. I want God to steer my meditations—my reflection time. Once I pray that verse, I trust that He will guide the ponderings of my heart when I dig to discover what pulls me or tempts me from His best.

God can reveal the origin of personal and inherited lusts. For some of us, it will be a traumatic incident. For others, it will be a circumstance or atmosphere that turned them off. For example, if a child's home life is chaotic, when they are an adult, they may subconsciously set out to control everything and everyone. This lust for control is the consequence of their childhood inability to deal with the chaos.

During your reflection time, you may remember that your uncle or mom dealt with the same issue. Maybe you will recall a family story. Perhaps you witnessed a relative being pulled away by the same lust. Remember, lust—the strong desire, can be for anything. Usually, we focus on the "big sins," but we can be drawn easily into anything contrary to the Lord—worry, self-soothing mechanisms, controlling others, etc. The enemy of our souls does not just want to hinder our progress, he wants to hinder a whole lineage. Being aware of inherited predispositions and partnering with God to undo them through mind renewal, willful surrender, and emotional healing can bring about release from these issues. Remember, the Holy Spirit will lead you. Philippians 1:6 is another verse that I often recite. Here are two versions.

> The enemy of our souls...wants to hinder a whole lineage.

...being confident of this very thing, that He who has begun a good work in you will complete it until the day of Jesus Christ
Philippians 1:6 (NKJV)

I'm fully convinced that the One who began this glorious work in you will faithfully continue to process of maturing you and will

put his finishing touches to it until the unveiling of our Lord Jesus Christ!
Philippians 1:6 (TPT)

Fact-Based versus Fear-Based Restrictions

The last section explained how James 1:14 teaches us that each human being has strong desires that they must acknowledge. Once a person is redeemed, the power of sin is broken; however, our minds can carry the memories and lure of those strong desires. Our memories are stores in a part of the brain called the amygdala. The brain and the mind are interconnected. One is physical; the other immaterial. As Christians, we have to acknowledge these strong desires so that we can ask God to renew our minds and revamp our brain's storage centers so that those temptations are no longer our own.

To give the next generation a head start, we can help our children and teens get to "know" themselves, that is, become aware of what lures them into moments of compromise. Eventually, they will come to a place where they can ask the Holy Spirit to undo mental, emotional, or genetic ties that bind them to unhealthy desires and behaviors. Our modeling will give them a vision of what the journey of becoming whole looks like.

Our modeling will give them a vision of what the journey of becoming whole looks like.

Parenting based on how our souls work and the facts of human development can help us to engage our children in gentle and honest, non-threatening conversations. Like Christian discipleship, parenting isn't meant to be rigid, overbearing, stoic, or impersonal. Imagine taking your daughter out for an ice cream sundae and sharing the challenges you had when you were her age. Share what God has taught or is teaching you about those challenges in retrospect. Explain the responsibility that God has given you and your spouse to keep your daughter safe, to help her understand life and get to know herself. Speak to her most true identity—the daughter that God envisions in His heart. Call her destiny forth, and let her know that sometimes, life is hard to live.

We won't be perfect, but our parental prayer to God can be, "Lord, help me be a safe refuge for my kids to show them that You are the safest refuge for us all. Help me be 'for them and not against them,' and for them to know it. Help me be their fortress and promote divine restrictions that are fact-based and not fear-based."

Governing Oneself

An elder in our former church co-led an organization that taught America's Christian history. I remember a talk he did about the term "self-governance." He shared that the task of every parent is to train their children in such a way that they will have the tools to govern themselves. This requires that they understand what Paul teaches about in Romans 8:7, that "the carnal mind is enmity against God; for it is not subject to the law of God, nor indeed can be."

Our children, even once they receive salvation, must understand the war that goes on in their thinking that will affect their words, emotions, and behavior. These components are the realm of the soul. As adults, we also need to be aware of this war. Paul teaches in Romans 12:1 that we are "transformed by the renewing of our minds." As we train our children and allow the Spirit of God to teach us, we are changing our thinking so that it will agree with the Word of God. All of us, parent and child, need to think as Jesus thought. The ability to self-govern will follow.

Modeling self-control to our children involves perspective and restriction. The Scriptures warn us about a time where "men will be lovers of themselves, lovers of money, boasters, proud, blasphemers, disobedient to parents, unthankful, unholy, unloving, unforgiving, slanderers, without self-control, brutal, despisers of good, traitors, headstrong, haughty, lovers of pleasure rather than lovers of God, having a form of godliness but denying its power." (2 Timothy 3:1-5) Yikes! Sounds like the world highlighted on reality TV and broadcast on the morning news. Scripture foretells a time where permissiveness runs rampant. It is not easy to balance giving our children enough freedom to let them learn through their mistakes yet protect them from what is beyond their stage of development. We have to train them to think through the heart attitudes of 2 Timothy 3:15 as they make choices. We can give them simple questions to ask themselves. *Why do I want to do this? When I choose to behave like this, what does it say about my thoughts, my will, or my emotions?* As we train them, we must not be afraid if they fail to make the best choice.

When I choose to behave like this, what does it say about my thoughts, my will, or my emotions?

God gives humanity the freedom to make choices. A decision either promotes or stagnates spiritual and emotional growth. So it is essential to train our children to look beyond immediate gratification and peer pressure and access the consequences of any choice. We should do this also for ourselves. But it can be hard to say no. Who wants conflict—with our kids or our flesh? Growing up, there were times my mom didn't give us a choice. She didn't fear our grumbling. We played outside for more hours than we watched TV. We read at least an hour a day. When we were bored, she'd give us ideas like listening and dancing to music, doing art or playing board games. We also had daily chores! She recognized that if she had not been proactive, our default would have been watching TV all day! Saying no is necessary. Likewise, self-restraint is a useful skill. It protects a child from running out into the street, hitting another child in anger or letting our lives revolve around our desires. As parents, we can order our lives in such a way that our family benefits, and we stay emotionally healthy.

No one likes legalism. Legalism is a strict, fear-driven mindset that can exalt man-made rules and undermine personal freedom. In an attempt to avoid being legalistic, we may allow ourselves and our kids to participate in things that negatively affect us-spiritually, emotionally, and physically. As I said earlier, as parents, we are not so quick to restrain ourselves at times -- the battle against over-indulgence is quite real. It may be food, alcohol, material goods—the list goes on and on of things that we may overconsume. Things like sports, a medical issue, or a friend's problems can consume us as well. Although none of these are sinful, all require self-control. We have to practice limits. We can avoid legalism by acknowledging things in life that are good and fun but also staying mindful of the value of a biblical moral compass and an understanding of the heart of the Father.

So be careful. Guard your hearts. They can be made heavy with moral laxity, with drunkenness, with the hassles of daily life. Then the day I've been telling you about might catch you unaware and trap you.
VOICE, Luke 21:34

We need to remind ourselves about the positive and negative influences that come through our five senses. We are to be the gatekeepers of our lives by paying attention to what goes in and what comes out.

Saying "no" and hearing "no" is difficult. Picture a scenario where co-workers or our peers are belittling someone. Because self-control involves safety, we can tell ourselves, "I am saying no to this unedifying conversation, and I am saying yes to protecting myself from the harm of gossip or slander." An unhelpful response is: "God commands me to not gossip or slander." The first promotes ownership of our wellbeing; the latter can instill a sense of being subjected to God's laws.

Cultivating the willpower to say "no" to ourselves takes more than a desire to please God. We need the realization that God adores us and wants our best. Saying "no" or "yes" to the right things will help us live fruitful and productive lives. He doesn't want us to spend more than our means. He wants us to get to work on time and exercise regularly. Self-control is the means to a good end.

In my upper-thirties, I realized that my self-control was the size of a grape. It needed to be a grapefruit! As a young mother, I'd been able to parent my first four children without having episodes of "losing it." I suppose my expectations of them were reasonable to their individual age and development. However, when they became teenagers, everything changed.

One of my sons played AAU basketball one summer. After a tournament as we drove home, I tried to hold my tongue, but it didn't work. I should have sat on it. Despite my intention to let him decompress in silence after his basketball game, I ended up giving him a ten-minute feedback session. In truth, it was a lecture. You'd think I'd get the hint when he put his jersey over his head. What was bubbling up so much in my thoughts and emotions that I couldn't honor my prior intention to hold my tongue? Why could I not control myself?

> I tried to hold my tongue, but it didn't work...why could I not control myself?

Out of the abundance of the heart, the mouth speaks. (Matthew 12:34) In other words, when we can't keep our mouths shut, we should realize that we are in a state of mental and emotional overflow. This can be good or bad, depending on what we are spewing from our mouths.

Often as parents, we end up parenting out of our own negative issues. It took me a few days to figure out why, no matter how hard I tried, I kept breaking a promise to myself to not give "parent lectures" at inopportune times. I would sense God nudging me to leave the child alone. But I ignored His still, small voice. I knew in my head that my son needed some moments to himself after the basketball game. I didn't think about the fact that God wanted to tend to my son's heart after this tough loss. My inopportune lecture interrupted God's plan for the car ride. Weeks later, after continually asking God to show me what was driving me, I realized that my son's success in athletics fed a subconscious desire in me for reputation. I wanted my son to be the star—the one who saved the day! In turn, I would feel important. So, when he didn't play as well as I thought he could, I was frustrated because his performance blocked my goal for reputation. This was subconscious, hidden in my blind spot, and God kept trying to turn my eyes inward so that I could see what was really motivating me. I was glad that God showed me that my frustration, disguised with a gentle tone, and covered up by good intentions, was affecting my son's relationship with me. Sometimes, when we dig deep, we discover those yucky parts of ourselves. Only then can we own our behavior.

God kept trying to turn my eyes inward so that I could see what was really motivating me.

In this case, I needed to pry even deeper to discover why I had a desire for reputation. In this journey of transformation, God mends what is broken within us.

Self-control also helps us achieve the future God has for us. He develops our self-control, diligence, and wisdom, to keep us from the distractions that hinder our forward movement and personal prosperity. We all love achievement. When we set our minds to a task and achieve it, neurotransmitters are released and give us a sense of joy and relief. Goal setting is advantageous, as long as our goals are attainable. Self-control is like the solid white lines on the highway, which help us stay on route to our destination and not wander off.

Remember when you were in kindergarten, and you had to learn how to color between the lines? This is a practical way to teach children how to refrain from going outside of preset boundaries. They also learn how to control the movements of their fingers. The process is developmental. It takes concentration. Such is the exercise of self-control. Boundaries are a blessing. Learning physical self-restraint is vital.

Act of the Will or Not?

Can we quickly choose self-control in a moment where our emotions are frayed, and temptations are triggered? Often not, and the reason helps us steer away from self-condemnation. We must understand how our souls work. Our souls comprise our subconscious and conscious mental and emotional processes. Some Bible verses use the word "heart" when discussing the storage place of our thoughts, intents, and motivations. The other aspect to our souls is the will—the place of surrender and initiative. This immaterial part of us needs more focus than we usually realize. More often than not, we focus on outward behavior. But the soul is the seedbed for our behavior.

Our souls comprise our subconscious and conscious mental and emotional processes.

Think of your soul as a mansion with various levels and many rooms. Some levels have an open floorplan, in other words, the spaces overlap. We can have one space in which our childhood memories reside. Another space has emotions associated with these memories. If some of these emotions are negative and have never been processed with Jesus, then hidden stress is carried into our present lives. The stress comes out when it's triggered.

No matter how much we pray and rehearse the scripture about being slow to speak when we are triggered we find that we can't control ourselves. We respond harshly. Without thinking. A bad day at work makes us act out by overindulging or caving into temptation. We want to control ourselves but find that we keep messing up. In these moments, let's place a yellow traffic light in front of us. This is an opportunity to slow down and ask God to show us why we keep tripping up. What is the trigger? What lies hidden in our souls that we haven't processed with Jesus?

What lies hidden in our souls that we haven't processed with Jesus?

I mentioned before that many of our predispositions can be genetic. Epigenetics is a field of science that studies what is passed down in the DNA. It's been amazing to learn that our DNA carries more than just physical information! We inherit patterns of behavior as well as emotional dispositions. What gets passed down can either be a strength or a weakness, a blessing or a curse. The strengths can be anything from athleticism and creativity to 20/20 vision.

As we take the time to discover why it may be difficult to have self-control, certain questions will naturally arise. These questions are helpful no matter what the sin or emotional tendency. When do I behave/feel this way? Did any of my parents or siblings ever behave/feel this way? If we realize that our tone of voice is often sharp, we can try to remember if either of our parents regularly spoke harshly to us. If feelings of loneliness are present more than absent, we can think about the relationships in our family of origin. Was there an emotional connection? If no, then why not? These last questions will be helpful to any of you who may have been adopted as children or in the foster care system. It can be helpful to get information about your birth parents. Whether inherited or imparted by our environment or childhood circumstances, a lack of self-restraint or any weakness can be overcome.

The Bible uses the word iniquity for a sin pattern that runs in the family line. You may have also heard the terms generational curse or generational iniquity. Simply, iniquity is a "bent" away from God's ways. It is carried through our bloodline. The journey towards wholeness involves us inviting the Spirit of God to show us anything in our souls that He wants to tend to. The more aware we are of the unseen parts of our humanity, the more we can appreciate the mysterious work of our Master Gardener.

The word heart is often used interchangeably with the soul. Proverbs 4:23 says, Keep your heart with all diligence, For out of it spring the issues of life. We must consider what issues lie hidden in our souls, in order to have the abundant life that Jesus desires for us.

Emotional Maturity

How do our emotions play a role in setting limits? I find that when I'm weary, I pick up my phone to play a game. The game removes me from anything that would draw on my almost depleted mental resources and make me aggravated. As we become self-aware, we will find that it becomes easier to detect our emotional gauge. We can teach our children to do the same. Usually, these teaching moments with our children come because of real experiences. For example, texting her boyfriend for hours may make our fifteen-year-old daughter happy, but her schoolwork remains unfinished. The next day, she finds out that her favorite store is having a sale, so she asks for an early allowance. When you remind her that she has enough clothes, she gets angry and goes on a verbal tirade. It could be hormones, but is there anything else behind her decision-making

How do our emotions play a role in setting limits?

and her intense emotions? As we regularly teach our children about the benefit of limits, we need to also teach them about their emotional gauge, what gives it fuel, and what depletes it. God wants to help them as they navigate their emotional landscape. Sometimes, our children's emotional needs can affect their ability to set limits. (The same goes for us!) If our daughter is depressed, texting her boyfriend is the emotional boost that she craves. It becomes like a drug and keeps her on a high. Shopping has the same effect. When that desire was blocked, she got angry. She needs to discover what is behind her depression in order to establish healthy and responsible limits.

Noah had a hard time controlling his fondness for alcohol. Many of us understand that a nice glass of wine after a hard day makes us relax. Certain types of wine help stomach ailments. Wine was used as a celebratory drink in Bible times. However, the Bible is clear about drunkenness, and Noah had a weakness in this department. *And Noah began to be a farmer, and he planted a vineyard. Then he drank of the wine and was drunk and became uncovered in his tent.* (Genesis 9:20-21) Noah got so drunk that he let it all hang out! Apparently, in this condition, his younger son disrespected him, although the Bible doesn't reveal the details of what happened. Mind you, this could have been a single incident in Noah's life. Unfortunately, his lack of self-control with alcohol consumption was presented to his son.

We teach our kids to keep their hands to themselves, but we also need to teach them to guard their eyes.

King David indulged his eyes too much, resulting in adultery and murder. Whether we like it or not, voyeurism in a myriad of forms is a problem in today's culture. We teach our kids to keep their hands to themselves, but we also need to teach them to guard their eyes. Eyes are gates. What you see is recorded in your brain. Images are seeds. As parents, we can use safeguards like parental controls, but we need to take time to explain to our kids what self-control looks like and how it benefits them and us.

Specific limits can be subjective from person to person, but God offers some truths to be our compass:

Finally, brethren, whatever things are true, whatever things are noble, whatever things are just, whatever things are pure, whatever things are lovely, whatever things are of good report, if there is any virtue and if there is anything praiseworthy, meditate on these things.
Galatians 4:8

Be slow to speak and quick to hear.
James 1:19

My son, hear the instruction of your father, and do not forsake the law of your mother; for they will be a graceful ornament on your head, And chains about your neck. My son, if sinners entice you, do not consent.
Proverbs 1:8-9

These scriptures reveal that God has given us the freedom to choose how we think, speak, and live. He tells us how to live in a way that promotes safety and mental, emotional, and physical wellness.

The War in Our Members

Who wants limits when the alternative feels good in the moment! Setting and practicing limits is a good exercise that will feel like an internal war sometimes. Paul refers to this war in Romans 7:23 when he writes, "...but I see a different law in the members of my body, waging war against the law of my mind..." We know better, but at the same time, we want to feel good. We want to be liked. So do our kids. God has given us the capacity to choose what we will orient ourselves toward in order to feel good or be liked. As parents, it exasperates us when our kids do something that we've taught them not to do.

"Why can't I hit him!" complains teary-eyed Jimmy.

"Because hitting doesn't solve problems. I've told you that before!" explains his mommy.

"But he hit me first!" shouts Jimmy.

"You should have told me and not take matters into your own hands. Did it feel good to hit him?" asked his mommy.

"Yes, real good!"

Jimmy is emotionally honest with his mother. He knows it's not right, but it felt good! Jimmy's problem was that his sense of justice was tied to responding in the way he was treated. When it comes to emotions, expressing them can feel good in the moment. However, we have to teach our kids and remind ourselves to find the best way to deal with a dilemma when our emotional gauge is reading "danger."

As a parent, talking with your friends about a teacher at your kid's school with whom some of you disagree may seem justifiable. It feels good to vent to someone who understands. After all, they share the same complaint. However, seeds of discord are sown when we do not examine the difference between venting and complaining versus discussing an issue with the right person to find God's resolution.

Self-control is often viewed in a negative light, but restraint is a wonderful attribute that has a great reward. In Luke 10, a woman named Martha was working hard to practice hospitality to Jesus. She was truly a servant who understood that she had a gift of hospitality. As often happens with us humans, she subconsciously projected her gift onto her sister Mary and complained that Mary was lazy.

Here is the story in Luke 10:38-42.

Now it happened as they went that He entered a certain village, and a certain woman named Martha welcomed Him into her house. And she had a sister called Mary, who also sat at Jesus' feet and heard His word. But Martha was distracted with much serving, and she approached Him and said, "Lord, do You not care that my sister has left me to serve alone? Therefore tell her to help me." And Jesus answered and said to her, "Martha, Martha, you are worried and troubled about many things. But one thing is needed, and Mary has chosen that good part, which will not be taken away from her."

Martha "welcomed Jesus into her home." I see graciousness and kindness in that wording. Martha was not put off by Jesus' company. She welcomed the one everyone knew as "teacher." When I used to read Jesus' response to her complaint, I would hear His tone as being harsh. However, Jesus always wants what is best for people. Was He giving a sharp reprimand or insightful advice? Did Martha realize that her good deeds were motivated by worry? In His response, Jesus shows Martha a soul issue. His compliment to Mary is not to shame Martha, but to give her perspective when it comes to temporary and eternal opportunities. Serving others is wonderful! Jesus appreciated her taking the opportunity to welcome Him into her home and serve Him. However, Jesus wanted her to take hold of a moment that would give her eternal food: the word of God. Martha would need to put aside the duties

In His response, Jesus shows Martha a soul issue...not to shame Martha, but to give her perspective when it comes to temporary and eternal opportunities.

and tasks that she functioned so well in. She needed to say no to her function and her mindset. She needed to show self-restraint and halt her activity in order to listen. Self-control means practicing limits even in good things that you have been wired to do to gain something greater.

Be Real with God in the Struggle

We all have issues. As we become self-aware and begin "working on" ourselves, we can get weary and feel like such a mess. We do what our counselor recommends, study church sermon notes, and pray. We try new things like kneeling on the floor with worship music playing and inviting the Holy Spirit to fill us anew. However, sometimes the changes in our personal lives and our families don't come fast enough. Frustrated, we wrestle with the tension of doing our part and giving time for God to do what only He can do.

> As we become self-aware and begin "working on" ourselves, we can get weary and feel like such a mess.

How many of us feel comfortable telling God that we are angry with Him for not moving fast enough? Neuroscience has taken strides in revealing the relationship between thought patterns and emotional honesty. We need to become comfortable being raw and transparent with Him. Emotional honesty in safe spaces promotes even physical health. God is safe.

Thessalonians 5:18 says, 'In all things give thanks.' Even when we are weary, or we experience a major failure with our teenager, we can thank God that someday there will be a silver lining. Is there anything you are condemning yourself for? Maybe, you had a goal to hold your tongue. But you didn't. Although you are moving toward it, the victory isn't present at this point in your journey. Keep your head up. Remember, there is a lesson gained at every turn. Take time to sit and listen. Realizing how much we need God's help makes us more conscious of His still, small voice and gentle nudging.

Self-control thrives in our lives as the Holy Spirit keeps us centered on Jesus Christ. We are less likely to react to our teen coming home an hour after her curfew when we have made it a habit to pause and discern God's counsel throughout our day. The Holy Spirit can impart divine perspective that gives us a broader vantage point in a given situation. Discernment and perspective will cool our tempers once they flare up, and they help us refrain from speaking until we know that our response would be God-approved. Wisdom comes through patience. A person with self-control will govern a family well.

The Expectation Ruler

We must understand how much we should fairly expect from our children during their various ages and stages when it comes to self-control and honoring set limits. Sometimes we can expect too little and keep the bar too low. When we hesitate before giving our kids a chore, debating whether we feel like dealing with their whines, the Holy Spirit wants to show us that we are not exerting our God-given parental authority. We must call their whining what it is: complaining. It is a sin. God will help us address this with them even when we are tired. He values a good work ethic and will give us the endurance to keep teaching our children the value and selflessness of household chores. Kids must learn how to obey without complaint. We have to learn to maintain our parental authority without hesitation.

Proverbs 1 expects a son to be trained to "not forsake the law of his mother." When we tell ourselves that "boys will be boys" when it comes to areas that require self-regulation, we cheat them from an opportunity to understand God's ways. Every situation is an opportunity to sow a seed. Let's remember that the Holy Spirit uses the smallest situations to cultivate the fruit of the Spirit. He supernaturally moves in the unseen parts of our humanity.

As we teach self-control, we can expect that three-year-olds will still whine at times, but we can train them to take a deep breath, pause, and think about how they feel. Then we can give them the words to describe how they feel. Self-control means ownership of our bodies and mouths. I firmly believe that even teenagers can embrace a sense of individual responsibility where they don't blame others for their poor choices.

Culture has dealt with the epidemic of sexual activity with young teens for a long time. We need to be real with our kids about surging hormones. At the same time, let's impart confidence to our kids regarding God's ability and power to help them refrain from any sexual activity until marriage. We are not perfect creatures. An overview of history reveals the constant battle of humanity to find and live out God's grace. But in our weakness, we can discover God's strength.

As Christians, how do we measure ourselves? What should we expect from ourselves? There are various measuring sticks out there, some based on peer comparisons; others based on relativist ideologies. I've found that if I measure myself with the divine intent of God, that I fall short. The good news is that my faith acknowledges a Creator that is not distant, but willing to nurture my growth and forgive my shortcomings. When it comes to developing self-control, I need to slow my daily pace so that I am conscious of His voice and power every day.

I decided to name this chapter Holy Restriction vs. Legalism because when it comes to the fruit of self-control, many Christians have been taught rules that have become a stumbling block to their vitality in Christ. The grace to grow in Christlikeness is undermined by a perception that God is watching their every move, waiting to punish them if they mess up! Instead of being a joy-filled child of God who basks in Jesus' unconditional acceptance, they become paralyzed. *Will I mess up? Will I do this right? What if I fail?* Rules given from the fear-based inclinations of the rule-giver misrepresent God, who nurtures both the wellbeing and the maturity of the recipient. A person who hears "do this" and "don't do this" and is not taught the helpfulness of the Holy Spirit will operate out of obligation toward man instead of devotion to Christ.

Prayer

Heavenly Father, I've never realized how complex we are as human beings. When I think about what needs changing in my life, what memories from my past still haunt me, as well as inherited dispositions that are not Christlike, I feel overwhelmed. Guide me to take time every day to be quiet with You, to let Your Spirit sift through my complexities and bring to my attention what to tackle first. Help me remember that I am not doing the work of changing by myself, but I am yielding to the work that You are doing to change me. You love me, and you want what is best for me. Thank You, Lord, for walking through this process with me and for what it means for my children. In Jesus Christ's name, I pray, Amen.

Quiet Time

Can you determine any underlying fears that influence your behavior, reactions, or your household rules?

In what situations is it hard for you to have self-control (self-restraint)? Ask God to show you any subconscious emotion, mindset, or trigger that propels you to react.

Have a time of thanksgiving and worship. You can play a favorite song, hymn, or sing to yourself.

Chapter Four

†

Faithfulness: Honor Your Words

One of my sons wanted a dog badly. When he asked for one, we still lived in a small apartment. Although it was on the bottom floor, with a decent size concrete area outside our door, and a large grassy area in the back of the building, I explained that we didn't have space for a dog. Our next home was a three-story townhouse. Technically, of course, we could have gotten a dog, but my feeling was that the common grassy area would mean that the dog would be tethered and unattended for a long period of time. I thought it would be best to wait until my son was older and we had our own yard.

Our next home was a 2400 square foot ranch on 1.7 acres. Believe me, I found an excuse. One of my younger children and my husband had begun having allergic reactions to certain animals—not dogs, but you never can tell, right? I also explained to this son that I really didn't have the desire to clean up after a dog. I told him that when I was a kid, my mom ended up taking care of the dog that my father brought home one day. When this son first asked, I knew in my heart that I didn't really want to care for a dog. I like dogs. But I don't like inconvenient messes.

Years later, I told him that I'd realized that my hemming, hawing, and lack of honoring my original words, "When you are eleven, we'll get a dog," hurt him deeply. I should have listened to his request and then really thought about it before answering. If I had, I would have told him "no" right then and explained the reasons which at that time were purely related to financial challenges and my unwillingness to be inconvenienced. I was trying to manage my household, and a pet would have been one more thing that I didn't want to think about.

He would have been disappointed, but at least he would not have wasted years hoping for something that was never going to materialize.

Faithfulness. Have you ever made a promise to your kids and didn't follow through? We have to remember that we need to explain matters honestly to our kids. I never wanted to let my kids know when we did not have enough money for something because I had a fear of them developing insecurities from our state of lack. However, that was my issue that I was projecting onto them. True, kids have to learn that money doesn't grow on trees and how to steward what you have even if it's small. They need to know that sometimes families experience economic challenges. When we tell our children the truth about difficult financial seasons of life, we are allowing God the opportunity to develop faith, hope, and long-suffering within their hearts. I learned too late that I should not promise what I am not sure I can deliver. All it takes is a conversation to explain to your child that your intentions for their joy are ever-present, but that you are not in control over the unexpected parts of life. My young boys get tired of hearing "maybe," but sometimes that is the best answer that I can give them.

So, what do we do with our guilt when we cannot follow through, and we feel like a failure? What can we do when we realize that the fruit of faithfulness isn't well developed, and we respond quickly and foolishly to appease the whines rather than allow our children to learn how to wait or live without?

God never wants us to take on guilt and self-condemnation. He desires to help us not only to view ourselves through His lens but also to teach our children how to have correct expectations of us as parents. On the one hand, it's nice to want to give our children everything that would make them happy. On the other hand, the need to prevent entitlement and selfish mentalities from taking root is important. When we realize that we have promised something prematurely, we can admit to our children that we make mistakes and apologize to them. We can share with them that sometimes we comment before truly considering the request.

Synonyms of faithfulness are dependability, stability, and loyalty. Do these words describe you? In what areas do they not? In our prayer times, we can ask God to tend to our emotional barrenness. We cannot give what we lack. Our all-knowing Creator who knows us better than we know ourselves forgives us and changes, comforts, and matures us. Acknowledging our frailties is the best thing we can do. It opens the door to wholeness.

Honing into the Bare Truth

Faithfulness keeps our hearts fixed on something that we deem essential. Sometimes we are more faithful to a friend or a boss than a spouse or a child. Single or married, our relationship with God is what anchors us to valuing this virtue in all of our relationships. Our children can learn to be faithful through our example.

Marriage begins with sacred vows that reflect the orientation of our hearts towards another person. The promise of faithfulness is meant to focus us mentally, emotionally, and physically on our spouse. I believe that the Bible teaches that God allows certain circumstances for ending a marriage, and one of them is infidelity. Many couples deal with the shame and the pain of this sin. Divorce might be an unfortunate consequence. It takes courage to share with your child or teenager, not the details, but the facts of your heart or their other parent's heart. We never want to shame a former spouse. That is rude and disrespectful. However, when a child is emotionally and mentally mature enough, they can understand the importance of faithfulness as being the key to maintaining a good relationship with another individual.

"I have not worked to keep a healthy relationship."
"I have been untrustworthy."
"I have broken promises."
"I have not been faithful to God."

These are all phrases that you can use with your teen or older child if you find yourself having to deal with divorce or separation or any type of relational unfaithfulness.

Faithful in the Small Things

Growing up in the 1970s and 1980s, my siblings and I had a great deal of responsibility as latch-key kids. We let ourselves in the house, started dinner, did chores, and finished our homework because that was the need and expectation of my mom. I remember the last time I got into trouble. It dealt with the area of dependability, which is related to faithfulness. I was eleven, and I sang in a city children's choir. We had four-hour rehearsals every Saturday. One sister and I were invited to a Friday night sleepover at a neighbor's house. I promised my mom to keep track of the time. Unfortunately, the next morning, when I finally looked at a clock, it was past the time needed to leave for rehearsal. I packed up in a hurry, and my sister and I ran to our house. It was my mother's turn to drive the other three girls that we carpooled with. My tardiness made all of us late for rehearsal. That evening, my consequence was one I care not to remember, but the virtue of faithfulness was forever etched in my soul.

How is faithfulness learned? Obviously, this attribute is a heart matter. We must have a heart that cares about how we steward our homes, our money, our relationships., and yes, our time. Another area is our words. The promises we make. Here's a paraphrase of Luke 6:45: *Out of the abundance of the heart, the mouth speaks.* Previously, I've mentioned the practice of listening to our words, what we say and how we say it. Once in a while, we need to figure out why we say what we say. Our words can reflect the state of our hearts—soil in our souls that needs cultivating. God wants to teach us to be faithful. First, He has to eliminate conditions that lead to unfaithfulness.

Our words can reflect the state of our hearts—soil in our souls that needs cultivating.

Our lack of faithfulness can appear subtly. For example, each time we sign up to volunteer at a church function, we cancel. We love our new jobs. The new house. But after the shine wears off, we cut corners at work or around the house. At home, instead of making sure our clothes are folded neatly, we fold them enough to just stuff them in the drawer.

When it comes to relationships, unfaithfulness can be subtle as well. Did your spouse ask you to do them a favor, and you forgot...again? Is this a habit? What thoughts can you trace that have formed opinions about your spouse or your kids that may cause you not to take their requests to heart? Our actions are linked to our thoughts and opinions. If you are like me, you love to have coffee dates with friends. Do you always show up a few minutes late or glance at your phone frequently during the conversation? Have you subconsciously begun to believe that your friends are annoying, and it is showing in your manner?

Our actions are linked to our thoughts and opinions.

The roots of unfaithfulness are watered by apathy. "I don't care." Most of us wouldn't admit this is the reason why sometimes we are unfaithful. But it hits the bitter truth. Sometimes we just don't care. We've become apathetic or passive in our souls. If we are honest with ourselves and with God, we will acknowledge where our hearts have grown cold.

In our immaturity, we can begin to ignore the details of what it takes to be dedicated to those around us. We hear our kids talk to us about their day at school, but we aren't actively listening to them. One response says, "I care about my own thoughts rather than your day," and the other says, "I choose to attend to you first." The truth is, living well and loving well can suffer when we live carelessly, forgetting the beauty of attentiveness and devotion. We can become so self-focused that we fail to esteem others, even our employers, ahead of our goals. A scripture like Colossians 3:23 sometimes doesn't carry the weight it should.

Whatever you do, do your work heartily, as for the Lord rather than for men.

Our salvation cry when we decided to follow Jesus was, "Yes, Lord! I'll serve you with all of my heart," but we didn't count the cost about what that would mean when we have a rude boss or have a job that we don't like. When the focus of our lives is ourselves, God and others will always be second place. We cannot be excellent and faithful stewards of our jobs, families, and communities if we are focused on what they do for us first. However, when our focus turns toward God—His purposes and His pleasure, a seed of devotion will implant itself in us. When we see God for who He is, we become dedicated to those He's entrusted to us. We will desire to do things that give Him pleasure. Yet, some of us have to go in a different direction to discover why we struggle to be faithful.

Has God Been Faithful to Me?

Sometimes we find that after we read about the importance of faithfulness, the information doesn't propel us into a fiery exuberance to serve God or others well. On one level, we want to serve because we understand that it's the right thing to do, and we know God wants us to do it. But when we try to "heartily" serve, the action is more obligatory than passionate.

The questions I propose to those of you who deal with this are, "Could you be affected by a subconscious belief that God hasn't been faithful to you? Why be loyal to Him when you are uncertain if He has been or will be faithful to you?"

God's word is truth and carries the power to change the human heart, but sometimes we read Bible passages or spiritual information through a jaded lens. Our experience has offered us a powerful accusation about God's heart that is difficult to destroy.

Lord, if You had been here, my brother would not have died.
John 11:21

These are Martha's first words to their close family friend, who happens to be the Light of the World, Jesus himself. Jesus was out of town when Lazarus, the brother of Martha and Mary, passed away. Martha knew that Jesus had healing power, and in their particular Hebrew tradition, they believed that resurrections could occur in the first three days of death. But Jesus arrived on day four.

Martha questioned His faithfulness even though she knew His power. "Why God?" is the echo of the ages. At the same time, embedded in Martha's words is a declaration about His heart. She knew that Jesus would have raised him. She knew that Jesus loved him and was serious about His divine mission to earth. Martha's first heart statement to Jesus is followed by a statement that shows us that despite her confusion about Jesus' delay, she knew His authority. *"Even now I know that whatever You ask of God, God will give you"* (v.22). For her to say something that directly opposed the tradition she'd been taught is remarkable. Again, this was day four. In her tradition, the priests didn't believe that resurrections could happen after day three. Most of you know the rest of the story from John 11. Jesus stuns the priestly community that had come to the funeral by resurrecting Lazarus on the fourth day. For Martha, the miracle didn't come in the time frame of her expectation. But it happened. God proved His faithfulness in a time frame and in a way that she didn't expect.

Each of us must come to a moment when we encounter God's heart for us and become convinced that He is for us, not against us. (Romans 8:38-39) We must pray for a God's eye view when we look back into past experiences that accuse Him of being unfaithful. As I share at another point in this book, my husband's *The God On Trial* series delves into the topic of accusations towards God, and I recommend it to anyone dealing with this area. In book two, *God: Accused or Excused,* Doug writes:

> If you believe that God wanted mankind to fall and suffer so that God's Son Jesus would have to come and be tortured as some master plan to save the world, that would make God sadistic against mankind and his Son, Jesus. However, if you believe God simply knew that mankind could choose to disobey like Lucifer and had a discussion with His Son about how mankind could respond, then you understand that His resoluteness of love and willingness to rescue is truly unimaginable. (26)

Doug's book goes through the first few chapters of the book of Genesis and helps readers learn that there is more to a situation than meets the natural eye. Our accusations against God end when we can see a bigger picture than we've ever seen before. God is faithful. The fruits of the Spirit are His attributes. He, the Father, sent His only begotten Son, Jesus, to be the Savior of broken hearts. Sin swept us away, but He swooped down as a human being to provide a way for our return. Jesus, the incarnate Christ, understands the pain that we experience but reveals the real enemy and bringer of pain. If you have a wounded heart, I pray that one day, God will convince you of His faithfulness. Then, your own faithfulness will flow as an unobstructed river.

Sin swept us away, but He swooped down as a human being to provide a way for our return.

Because God desires us to live faithfully and do our tasks heartily (Colossians 3:23), a whole, healed heart's answer is an immediate "Yes!" His desires become a higher priority than our own.

Even if your work involves tedious data entry, service calls to grumpy homeowners, unproductive meetings, or managing staff conflict, it's worth it. Dot your "I's" and cross your "T's" in everything that you do. This is the heart of the faithful.

Someone once asked me for an example of how my kids have learned about faithfulness from my example. I was honestly dumbfounded with the question. It was weeks before I could give an answer. Finally, as I thought about it at the dinner table one evening, I concluded that the only thing I could think of was my prayer life. Nothing has ever, nor will ever keep me from prayer. They see me pray while washing dishes, folding laundry, driving, and even while I write! As I grew to understand the power of prayer, my love for it increased. Instead of kissing an "ouchie," we pray over it. Instead of blowing out a candle and "making a wish," we pray over the birthday person and bless them with scriptures or other kind words that God puts on our hearts for them. I would say that my faithfulness to pray has taught them that self-reliance is contrary to our Christian identity. We need God. Prayer is our active, sincere demonstration of this fact.

For I know the plans that I have for you,' declares the LORD,
'plans for welfare and not for calamity to give
you a future and a hope.
Jeremiah 29:11

Prayer

Lord, I am humbled as I realize how important the fruit of faithfulness is in life. Sometimes, it's hard to admit that I have not been faithful as I know I should. I see that I don't value commitment and dedication as You do. I'm sorry. Holy Spirit, move fully in my soul and bring the fullness of repentance. While I intellectually admit my error, sweep through the soil of my soul: memories, personal experiences, and even generational sin patterns. Heal me where my conscience has been seared and where apathy has begun to grow. I'm so grateful that you are a God that forgives. I end this prayer, not condemning myself, but boasting in You, God, who can do what my humanity cannot. I want to begin again. Take my spirit, my soul, and my body…it's all Yours. Take my spouse and my kids, every part of them, and begin the beautiful work of growing the fruit of faithfulness. Thank You. I pray this in the name of Jesus Christ, my Lord, and Savior.

Quiet Time

Think of one item that this chapter has taught you.

Write down or think about instances where you have been hurt by someone's unfaithfulness to you. Did you push the hurt aside or acknowledge it during a time of prayer? Jesus weeps with those who weep.

Have you extended forgiveness? Ask God to help you surrender your will and make this decision.

Chapter Five

Love Suffers Longer Than We Desire

In the late summer of 1999, my life was a mess. Literally. I sat on our second-hand sofa nursing child #4 with a pile of clean unfolded laundry next to me. The other three kids were hidden in a pile of toys on the floor in front of me. Dishes overloaded the sink. Beds were unmade, and the toilets of our bottom floor apartment needed cleaning. Like every mother of a newborn, I was exhausted and emotionally frazzled. Lots to do and little energy. My kids and husband relying on me to meet their basic needs.

When I had my fourth child, my husband worked two jobs. Sometimes three. Bless his hard-working heart! It was cheaper for me to stay at home than to pay for daycare, and eventually, we wanted to home school. At this particular time, we also had custody of a nephew and a niece who were 15 months and 2 ½ years old, respectively. I was so thankful for compassionate ladies in my church that came over to help when they could. But daily life was clouding my vision. Envisioning my future was like staring into a dark abyss. I had been the oldest child and a neighborhood babysitter. So the tasks of motherhood didn't overwhelm me. I loved to cook and make up stories to entertain the kids. What overwhelmed me was the day-to-day fight between my perfectionist mentality and the abundance of daily tasks. Also, I had deep soul wounds that I didn't know how to close. I'd lost two babies from miscarriages years before, and my marriage was in the throes of financial stress and personality clashes. I adored being a mother, but the challenges of motherhood were showing me how impatient and harsh I could be. I needed a serious dose of divine long-suffering and a good night's sleep.

I had deep soul wounds that I didn't know how to close.

The year 1999 was more than twenty years ago. Now I have six children. My oldest is twenty-eight, that nursing baby is now twenty, and our youngest is eight years old. Instead of dealing with toddler temper tantrums, my husband and I now engage in sobering, culturally relevant conversations with four single African American adults and pour ourselves into raising our two youngest boys. I'm now 50 and my 20-year stint as a homeschooling mom ended in 2017. Despite being parents for almost 30 years, raising kids still isn't a walk in the park.

My dad passed away in 2017, and since then, I've been meditating on how to persevere through seasons of suffering. One of the fruit of the Spirit is long-suffering or patience, which ties closely with the word *perseverance.* Pressing through when we want to give up. Endurance. The Merriam-Webster dictionary defines perseverance as "the continued effort to do or achieve something despite difficulties, failure, or opposition; steadfastness."

Suffering comes in different forms and degrees. I know of parents who have been struck with depression or ended their lives through suicide. I know of dads who have walked out the door and never looked back. There is the suffering of financial stress or the inconvenience when the car breaks down. Suffering occurs when a community faces divisiveness, a child is bullied, or when a loved one dies. Of course, we can suffer needlessly as well. I'm referring to the suffering that is the consequence of our own bad choices. We all have a list of those, don't we? When we knew better...but we made the wrong choice anyway!

As I grow older, I think more about the suffering that God never intended for mankind to experience in the first place. This is the suffering brought about by poverty, disease, or crime. God never intended for Cain to kill his brother. The crime happened, and Adam and Eve suffered a new level of loss. These plights have ransacked the world. Governments, organizations, and compassionate people all over the globe work to try to fix these conditions and improve people's lives so that they don't have to suffer. But in our fallen world, whole systems are corrupt, and I believe that only supernatural intervention—the power of God, can change things on that large of a scale. Until then, we will face suffering that God does not like.

How Well Do You Persevere?

As parents, our need for long-suffering is always before us. Child training is not the wondrous, adrenaline rush of goals set and quickly achieved. It is arduous, teeth-gritting, tongue-holding work that sometimes makes us wonder what life would be like if we'd never had children. Let's be candid and transparent. We've got to be real to be whole. I'll be the first to admit that I love my kids, but there have been times where they exasperated me so much that I had to leave the room to find where my love had run to!

It is arduous, teeth-gritting, tongue-holding work...

How we deal with the daily stress of parenting, as well as unexpected crises that arise, reveals the wholeness of our souls. I learned long ago that both suppression and indiscriminate reactions are unhealthy. If we go on a tirade at home or become emotionally erratic, we are reacting indiscriminately. When we deny that we are hurt, we are suppressing the pain. Often, we volley from one to another. How should we suffer—persevere through hardship?

Grieving is the key. We must sincerely acknowledge, and I daresay, live in our pain to get beyond our pain. We have to admit how we feel in the midst of daily stress, suffering, and trial. The end of 2017 was the beginning of my season of becoming acquainted with the grieving process. To go through various life changes well, I had let myself shake grief's hand and shed my tears on its shoulder. Not only was my dad's death unexpected, but people that I loved deeply were moving away. I suffered by having to deal with sleeplessness. Deep heartache. Confusion. Sometime during that long season of grieving, I wrote this in my journal:

We must sincerely acknowledge, and I daresay, live in our pain, to get beyond our pain.

Grief has ransacked my soul
Pommeled my heart into bitter pulp
I cannot feel the sun's feeble warmth in the winter skies
Just the 100-pound weight in my chest.

Some of you understand. You are there right now. I'm sorry that you can't sleep and enjoying life is the furthest thing from your mind. You are sad, devastated and that is okay. It is normal. On this side of heaven, we cannot escape sorrow that sometimes feels debilitating. A friend betrays you. Your teenager makes unhealthy decisions. You are turned down for a promotion. Yes, we suffer just through living.

I mentioned that the last half of 2017 was difficult for me due to family changes and my dad's death. My city was also dealing with a lot of racial turmoil that made my heart heavy. Two years before the previous incidents, I had a friend who was fighting cancer. She had six kids also, and as an older mom, she'd encouraged me when I'd become pregnant with my fifth child at age 40. Our oldest sons graduated from college on the same day. The day after these graduation ceremonies, her health plummeted, and she became hospitalized. She'd call me to pray with her on the phone a couple of times a week until she became too sick for phone calls. My heart ached for her. She wanted to live, which made her suffering emotional as well as physical.

It's hard to see a loved one in pain, let alone experience pain ourselves. I used to be embarrassed to cry in front of anyone, especially my kids. But in this situation, my oldest kids knew my friend and her children. While the whole process of grieving wasn't something that I'd fully understand until 2017, I knew enough to permit my kids to grieve openly by setting the example. I cried. I didn't try to smile for a couple of days. It would have been fake. All of us must become acquainted with the grieving process. We need to let it be okay to be emotionally honest in our homes. The length of time it can take to recover from an overwhelming experience. Understanding the importance of long-suffering helps us not rush through the process in order to escape the pain. We learn to process our pain amid our daily lives. Dishes still need to be washed, but sometimes our tears will mix with the running water. All of those trials helped me learn how to grieve. It's not easy and it's not a quick process. But the process heals the pain.

Dishes still need to be washed, but sometimes our tears will mix with the running water.

Some people suffer because of the life-controlling issues of a family member. This is not God's will. Whether it's an addiction or an emotion like anger, God never wants a family to suffer because a member becomes physically or emotionally abusive. We should never just "take it". Enabling does not help. Staying silent to maintain an outward family image will eventually cause a family to implode. Boundaries, intervention, or mediation are sometimes necessary to help the offender get the healing they need.

Life can just be hard. Suffering is everywhere. Some nights, when sleep is slow to greet me, my heart looks upward to see and to hear what God is doing and saying in so many situations on this topsy-turvy planet of His. We need the fruit of long-suffering to help us firmly set our feet to plod through the challenges we face.

Our Perspective in Moments of Trial

The story of Gideon demonstrates the importance of perspective when we face a challenge. Gideon repeatedly needed God to prove to him that his divine assignment—to overthrow the Midianite, would be successful. A few times, God acknowledges Gideon's fearfulness, but neither rebukes him nor trivializes the challenge of this young Israelite. The Midianites were formidable warriors. God repeatedly adjusts Gideon's perspective from what man can do, to what He will do, to develop his faith. Faith is the evidence of what we cannot see.

Faith is an important ingredient in longsuffering. It holds onto an expected end (Jer. 29:11, KJV). There are trials, some intense and others trivial by comparison. But how well we lean into God's comfort will dictate how well we persevere.

How well we lean into God's comfort will dictate how well we persevere.

Have you ever considered how the father of the prodigal son processed his trial? Another title for this bible story could be, The Longsuffering Father. The son had been asking for his inheritance for a while—which amounts to saying, "Dad, I wish you were dead." Can you imagine how this emotionally affected his father? Yet he endured the immature insistence of his son. He had a perspective that helped him endure. I think he knew that his son needed to come face to face with his brokenness. His sinful nature. So the young man gets the early inheritance and flounders it. While he was gone, his dad must have endured a range of human emotions, yet he had faith. He continually watched for his son's return. How could he have been so sure—so expectant, regarding the end of this trial? I believe this dad trusted in the love of God to bring his son to maturity. Faith sees God working things out.

Perspective Helps Us Let Go

Perspective helps us pick our battles. We cannot tackle everything at once. One of my sons was the perfect angel until it came time for potty-training. His adamant nature snuck up on me one day. He frowned at the Elmo toilet insert I bought. And in his opinion, the other training potty was only useful for standing on to brush his teeth. My other sons were closer to three years old when they decided that potty-trained was a worthwhile endeavor. I suppose I should have been encouraged that at least this one stood next to his older brother to watch and study the standing up option. Although various cultural traditions, some experts, and other daycare-attending toddlers prove that a 2½-year-old boy can relinquish his disposables, pull-ups, or cloth diapers, I decided to wait until this one was willing. I was not going to force the next stage of his life. I knew that it would come. Until then, my long-suffering came by opting to still change his diapers.

The process of childrearing includes trials, big and small. Some of them are self-inflicted because we can care too much about other people's opinions. This was me in potty training that particular child. I had to stop caring about other people's successes so that I wouldn't feel like a failure. I had to ask myself, "Who am I trying to impress?" Other times, I would consider, "In the scheme of time, how important is this issue right now?" Some trials are circumstantial. It's hard to be a single parent, a stay-at-home mom, or a professional that works all day, picks up the kids from daycare or school, and then be mentally and emotionally present until bedtime.

Perspective comes when we survey our current landscape and discover what to focus on. Maybe you are recently divorced. Now that you have to work, you have occasions where your six-year-old needs to stay with relatives after school. The problem is that he just started misbehaving in school and you are trying to figure out methods of discipline or appropriate consequences to make him behave. But discipline may not be the route through this trial. You may have to focus on his heart for a while. Confusion and grief over the divorce may be the root of his behavior.

Focusing on what is most important helps us get through the stressful days and sleepless nights. The trials that seem endless. The space between dinner and bedtime when we want to unwind but our kids' behavior unravels. Perspective in these moments does help our fruit of the Spirit mature. We learn to lean on God. We get many opportunities to try to "get it right" when it comes to a godly response. A few years ago, I was glad to realize that the toddler tantrums, the pubescent mood swings for both males and females, the whining, and even the dishes left in the sink by one of my adult children, didn't raise my frustration to 212 degrees in two seconds anymore. Over time we can become less frustrated because we have learned what to expect with our days, which battle to focus on, and that sometimes we just need to let go of our version of the "ideal" evening.

Why Impatience Is Unfair to Our Kids

Some Bible versions use the word "patience" instead of long-suffering. Honestly, I can be so impatient when it comes to waiting for my kids to be responsible, self-governing children who clean up after themselves without being told and make sure they didn't leave the toilet roll empty. I know some of you can relate!

I have found that when I'm repeating myself, nagging and reminding my young Padawans of what they need to do correctly, I have to take a step back and say to myself, "Do I need to stop reminding them and allow them to experience the repercussions of their inaction?" Another question I have to ask myself is, "Have I explained to them the ramifications of their action or inaction in a way that they understand?"

Once we answer these questions we can realize why it is unfair for us to be impatient when they are not changing. It's on us when we don't take the time to explain the cause and effect of their decisions or remind them that actions have consequences. As parents, we can get lazy in our training and discipline. We can get soft when we need to stay firm. Why? The Holy Spirit invites us to investigate what is going on in our minds or our emotions that may cause us to be lax in our parental authority. It takes determination to execute a consequence. Such as saying, "No more playing cards with me" when your ten-year-old daughter either whines when you win or cheats to make sure she wins. You must remain firm and not back down even though she may frustrate you by whining even more.

The Holy Spirit invites us to investigate what is going on in our minds or our emotions that may cause us to be lax in our parental authority.

Before setting a boundary or dishing out discipline, God has taught me the importance of taking the child aside to talk about issues of the heart. During these times, I may have to turn the stove off or give another child an activity to do, because these conversations take time. I can't rush through them if I want fruit to come from them. Often, I don't quite know what to say or how to teach my child about the root of their behavior. In these conversations, John 14:26 comes to life.

But the Comforter, who is the Holy Ghost whom the Father will send in My name, He shall teach you all things…
John 14:26

Before I had kids, I only had an intellectual understanding of this verse. But God has amazed me on the spot so many times. He became my present help when I was in need and helped me counsel my child on how to become aware of their brokenness. Ways of explaining biblical truth, illustrations and metaphors come to my mind that I would never have thought of in my capacity. I've watched Doug counsel a child and seen the "aha" in their eyes.

In addition to having these conversations, I encourage you to also pray over them and lead them in prayers of confession. Then remind them that 1) the repercussions of their misdeed, 2) renewing their minds, and 3) grasping how much God and you will always love them will help them begin to change. Lasting change only comes when their hearts are changed by the transforming love of God. Let's be patient with them as they grow just like God is patient with us.

Let's be patient with them as they grow just like God is patient with us.

Appreciate Teenage Discovery

Raising our teens can seem like an "us versus them" battle. However, it should be a "we" journey. And the word journey expresses the need for long-suffering. We love the mountain peaks, but we must appreciate the mudholes. We remember what our teen years were like, don't we? Our Adolescent Story. Attitudes were like mosquitoes in a swamp… everywhere! One of the most memorable things my mom said to me when I was seventeen was: "Tina, you have to remember that you are my first.

I've never done this before." Her honesty rocked me. It revolutionized my perception of her. For the first time, I saw my mom as a human being, not just as "mom." It changed my attitude and reactions toward her forever. Teens just need perspective.

Society gives a perpetual viewpoint that teenagers are troubled and troublesome. Sure, the developmental stage of adolescence is challenging, but we can help our teens foster a healthy self-concept. As a teenager, Jesus must have had a good perception of himself. Scripture reveals that when he was twelve, he was comfortable enough with his identity and purpose to teach in the temple. If our teens have professed faith in Christ, then they are no longer sinners chained to sin but saints who struggle to resist the enticements of sin. They are the King's kids! No longer slaves but sons who have inherited the nature of their Creator through supernatural redemption. If our teens have yet to give their lives to Christ and are searching, we can remind them that they are created in the image of God. Created with a purpose. Known by God before they were conceived. He loves them. Their self-concept must be centered on how God sees them, not their behavior or even their feelings. Before Jesus did any miracle or preached the gospel, the Father affirmed His sonship. God values relationships more than performance or actions.

Their self-concept must be centered on how God sees them, not their behavior or even their feelings.

One way we can help our teens persevere through those years is to help them refrain from identifying themselves by their behavior. "I'm a failure". They are not failures. We all fail at times, but the Bible says, we are more than conquerors in Christ Jesus (Romans 8:34-37). Like us, teens need to understand the realm of the soul. We have to teach them the functions and purposes of their feelings and their will, their thoughts and their physical bodies. They need to be self-aware. If they can decipher the pull of their emotions or the effects of hormones on their brains, they will be better equipped to persevere through adolescence.

Let's make adolescence a joint adventure of discovery. Make time for focused conversations. Ask our teenagers their opinion about something. Once they know that they have been heard, we can share ours and even more importantly, we can invite them to find God's perspective about that topic with us.

Matters of sexuality, romance, and sensuality are confusing these days. I believe what C. S. Lewis writes in *Mere Christianity*: "God became man to turn creatures into sons: not simply to produce better men of the old kind but to produce a new kind of man." Let's raise a new kind of teenager. One who recognizes that God's design for sex has a unique purpose and value. That a relationship with Christ will give them a proper identity of themselves. These issues are delicate but normal.

Hopefully, if their Christian identity is established through God's lens, then sexuality and sexual expression will be discovered at an age-appropriate time when their mindsets, their emotional capacities, and their physical bodies are ready for the union of marriage. There are unfortunate spiritual, emotional, and sometimes physical consequences when engaging in the beautiful invention of sexual intimacy outside of marriage. While waiting for the ordained time and covenant relationship, our teens and young adults will experience the suffering that comes with emotional and physical longing.

Consider it nothing but joy, my brothers and sisters,
whenever you fall into various trials.
Be assured that the testing of your faith [through
experience] produces endurance
[leading to spiritual maturity, and inner peace].
And let endurance have its perfect result
and do a thorough work,

so that you may be perfect and completely developed [in your faith], lacking in nothing.
James 1:2-4 (AMP)

I adjure you, O daughters of Jerusalem, that you never [again attempt to] stir up or awaken love until it pleases.
Song of Solomon 8:4 (AMP)

This Old Testament book delves quite beautifully into the intimate relationship between a husband and wife. Some of the metaphors are quite descriptive and may make you blush. This Song of Solomon verse teaches many things, but one that I learned is that no matter what society thinks, there is an age where human beings are too young to be "awakened" to the experience of sex, sexuality, and romance.

We can help our sons and daughters become emotionally and spiritually mature men and women, who turn to God for strength and patience while they await the grand day of a marriage ceremony. During the journey, they will find that He is gracious, wise, full of compassion, and endowed with supernatural power. We can affirm their legitimate hormonal desires and pray for them to have endurance and mental strength. It won't be easy in today's world. But we can pray for healthy outlets to make the waiting easier.

When my teens were around sixteen, I told them about an excellent ministry, Moral Revelation, to make sure they had access to topics that I didn't cover well or mention at all. I made sure that this website was Christ-centered but candid about these topics. In today's world, we must grow comfortable discussing controversial issues. Among these are dating and emotional development, God's view of our sexually stimulated culture, the Bible's basis for heterosexuality, and how the covenant of marriage is the only permissible time to engage in sexual expression. In Christian circles, it is easy to assume that everyone has the same views. However, the array of topics brings an array of opinions. A topical bible study with our kids is a good way to hone in on what God thinks about a topic.

Some of you reading have been comfortable talking about these topics and subtopics with your children face to face. Bravo! Others of you realize that these topics are beyond your comfort zone. Don't condemn yourself. Find out why these topics are uncomfortable for you. Maybe this will be an area where God wants to help you. Truth is, our kids are hearing a whole lot! As our children get older, it's normal for these topics to come up with their friends, but let's make sure they hear from us as well. Let's remind our kids that their maturing peers aren't experts yet.

Mind you, the best model and teaching for our kids about romance and sexuality is the marriage relationship. What do your kids see when you are with your spouse? Is there affection and emotional security? In contrast, if you are a single or divorced parent, are you able to be transparent with your teens about your life experiences and human longing yet point them to God's desire that marriage is the boundary for physical intimacy?

Human sexual health is as necessary as physical, emotional, mental, and spiritual health; our kids need to grow up understanding this. But marriage is the boundary line. God said it is best this way.

Love Suffers Long

We fight for what we love. Persist in what is important to us. Longsuffering—perseverance keeps us from giving up. Those who persevere stay hopeful because they keep God as their main focus. God gives us perspective through trials and endurance as we navigate times of pain. In my area, there have been four suicides that I have heard about. In the past few years, our nation has been ransacked by shootings, racism, and violent protest. You may have friends who just experienced a miscarriage, a lay-off, or a family death due to a drunk driver. Death's defeat was secured by Jesus upon His resurrection, but yet, we see death's dance in the daily news over and over again. Life is precious, worth fighting for, and we must realize that while we have breath, it's necessary to fasten ourselves to God's priorities for our lives. Faith and family are high on His agenda. Faith is the foundation that cannot be shaken, no matter what storm, what disease, or what murderous rampage attacks our communities. The family is the building block of healthy communities, and in turn, a life-giving society. But to maintain both of these, faith and family, we have to learn how to embrace the issue of suffering and deal with it God's way.

At what times do we use the offense armor of Ephesians 6:10-19 to repel suffering that the enemy wants to bring? After all, Scripture says in John 10:10 that the enemy wants to steal, and to kill, and to destroy. This is important to think about because as I stated at the beginning of the chapter, there is suffering that God doesn't want for us. God wants us to make the right choices so that we don't suffer needlessly. At the same time, we were born into a world of sin and evil. Systems are corrupted by sinful people. Proverbs 29:2 says "When the righteous are in authority, the people rejoice; but when the wicked rule, the people groan." This is suffering that God doesn't like. Unfortunately, it's not easily solvable, and as a result, we do suffer.

We need perspective these days—like the Longsuffering Father who held onto the fact that God is always at work in the lives of those we love. At the same time, we bring our fears and questions to God with the transparency of Gideon.

We need to be free to grieve. Divorce happens and teens rebel. Kids have tantrums in the grocery store which makes us feel helpless and embarrassed. A young man in our community is shot. We need to acknowledge our anger. Weep when we feel helpless.

Groan when we feel weary. While the many degrees and types of suffering require perspective and faith in God to guide us through, our minds and our emotions need the process of grieving to endure the trials that make life overwhelming.

As we raise kids in today's world, we can be uncomfortable with the hard situations that they face. How can we expect our children to deal with suffering and cultural chaos if we haven't taken the time to process this stuff? The media will give them answers based on the paradigm of a particular news outlet. But we are their parents. We are their primary authority figures. We need to fine-tune our perspectives of events in the world. As we do, let's remember to look up and beyond the disarray of this human experience and set our eyes on a kingdom that has no end, a kingdom whose ways transcend natural comprehension. With divine perspective, long-suffering comes more easily.

Prayer

Holy Spirit, come. Fill me. Father, forgive me for the times when I lean to my own understanding. Help me to acknowledge You in everything I do and to follow Your direction. I want more endurance. Develop this through the trials that come, even the ones that I bring into my life when I fail. When the enemy attacks my family and me, help us use the sword of the Spirit, which is the Word of God, even as Jesus did when he was tempted by the devil in the wilderness. Your Word is powerful. Help me teach my children how to war against the enemy as he works through culture, through people, or through situations to kill, steal, and destroy the wonderful destiny that You have designed for them. Thank You for being there for us even when we are weak. Put safe people around us that can encourage us when we can't see the Your expected end. Also, bring safe people to us when we simply need to cry. Continue to remind us of the need to set aside time alone with You, in prayer, worship, and study. Thank You, God. I pray this in the name of Jesus.

Quiet Time

Ask God to show you any areas of your kids' souls (mind, will, emotions) that need healing, restoration, or renewing. Pray some scripture verses over your child.

Do you wrestle with a life-controlling issue whether it's an addition or an emotional tendency like worry? Ask the Holy Spirit to uproot them and repair your soul. He is your Deliverer and your Healer. Ask Him to send mature, humble believers to help you.

Chapter Six

The Spirit of Gentleness

Years ago, I realized that I was majoring in the little things when it came to household "rules". Instances of a towel being left on the floor and dishes left in the sink instead of loaded in the dishwasher would set me off. The forgotten chore and the carton of juice placed back in the refrigerator when it only had an ounce left in it would produce an angry reaction. While these things were certainly signs of inattentiveness, they should not have brought me a level of harshness that surprised even me at times. I was treating these blunders like major offenses. Forgetting to put the toilet seat down is not as important as repeatedly breaking curfew, but my reaction would have made you think otherwise. God showed me that the fruit of gentleness was extremely undeveloped as my kids went through normal moments of inattention.

What drove me to make mountains out of molehills and to turn pet peeves into battles of "my way versus your way"? I had to find out. What is my personality? A learned response to inconvenience? I began to seek the Lord because I realized that what mattered more than the inconvenient habits of family members was my relationship with them.

Relationship: the intertwining of hearts, and experiences, and mission. Human bonding is meant to reflect the bond within the Godhead, which is unified and life-giving. None of us can prosper in a family atmosphere of relational dissonance, where tension is palpable and avoiding interaction becomes the norm. We are meant to thrive, to enjoy the pleasure of belonging. We should know that harmony at home will alleviate the stresses we face on the job or at school. But to foster this atmosphere, neither inconvenient habits nor pet peeves can be so important to us that they bring a wedge in our bond.

You may have a different issue that stifles gentleness in your life. As with the other spiritual virtues, any lack in our lives reveals a need for us to ask God what makes us get "out of the Spirit" in certain situations. What is the dam—the issue that stops the flow of these spiritual virtues of God—in this case, gentleness toward our kids and our spouse?

Rewiring Our Manner

There are occasions when I realize that how I want something done is based on my personality or how I'm wired. I know that I am administrative and task-oriented. I have had to realize that some of my kids are phlegmatic and relational. Finishing a text conversation or the chapter of a book may take precedence over my request for them to put their shoes in the mudroom. (After all, the shoes in the middle of the room aren't stealing their peace—like they are mine!) It helps to remember that our kids may be wired differently and see situations through a different lens. In this example, a clean house gave me peace, therefore it became a goal. When my goal was blocked by people not doing the tasks that would lead me to peace, I got harsh.

In my digging, God had to take me deeper into the soil of my soul. What does a clean house have to do with peace? I spent time with the Lord and realized that moments of chaos as a child bred in me the need to find peace in what is orderly and confined within outlined boundaries. Chaos equals disorder, therefore, a clean house is a symbol of order. One further word about personality. We cannot use our personality—how we are wired—as an excuse for our manner. I've heard people refer to type-A personalities as naturally domineering and unfeeling. God gave people like this a certain personality, but it must be reflective of God's character and the fruit of the Spirit. All of us, no matter what personality we have, need to submit to God's process of rewiring, renewing and adjusting in this journey toward emotional wholeness.

We cannot use our personality—how we are wired—as an excuse for our manner.

The other part of rewiring, or changing our manner is to review how well we communicate with our family members. Sometimes I've realized that I didn't communicate my preferences or expectations well, like where clothes are placed when removed from the dryer. (A chair is better than the floor!) If you are familiar with the book series by Peggy Parish about the character Amelia Bedelia, you'll know that the comedy of this character involves her taking her boss too literally. If her boss said, "Help me pack my suitcase. I need to catch a plane", Amelia Bedelia would wonder why her boss would want to run after a plane to catch it! The book conveys that how we communicate with others sometimes has to cater to the way they think—their wiring. I had to learn to be honest about what cleanliness did for me emotionally and clear about my preferences for various household details and chores.

Some of you can relate. These examples may seem petty to others of you, but our personalities and our expectations will affect our display of gentleness. What should be a gentle request for a clean bedroom before leaving in the van for a family vacation comes out as a harsh indictment: "You always leave your bed unmade!" On the other hand, a gentle and emotionally honest request would be "It gives me peace of mind when I come home to a clean house, so please check your room before we depart."

It is helpful to keep personality differences and developmental limits in mind in regards to our kids. If we are wired to be a go-getter and have strong leadership skills, and our fourteen-year-old doesn't want to pursue various school extracurricular activities, then we may get pushy and discontent. Similarly, when our young children don't listen or they interrupt us, we can snap in frustration if we don't understand what is normal for that stage of development. Young children have shorter attention spans. There's nothing we can do to change that. Expectations need to be dictated by the wisdom of God and our manner needs to reflect the Spirit of God no matter what our personality type.

Like a shepherd He will tend His flock, In His arm, He will gather the lambs and carry them in His bosom; He will gently lead the nursing ewes
Isaiah 40:11

Busyness, the Gentleness-Killer

Time can be our friend or our enemy. If we honor its brevity, it's our friend. We'll realize that the eighteen years of raising kids is brief compared to our total lifespan. Time becomes our enemy when we are focused on our own daily agendas and life goals and drift away from the responsibilities of raising kids. When we are busy and don't welcome space for the spontaneous child training moments that inevitably will occur, we will be harsh and impatient.

Gentleness emerges in an atmosphere of tranquility and ease. Parents, we need to slow down. Put our phones away. Cut down on activities. Make space in our days to sit and talk with our kids.

A child's understanding is like a pan of sauce that slowly simmers on the stove. It takes time to develop. What a fantastic experience it is to see the spark of understanding in our child's eye or witness them grasp the significance of the Cross after a conversation. Let's slow our busy lives. When we slow down, we can appreciate the process that our children are going through. A gentle shepherd leads his sheep by gentle waters, not rushing rivers.

Called to Be A Shepherd

What does gentle look like to you? You may have to give yourself a few minutes to think about this and I encourage you to do so. I picture scenes in nature. A stream as opposed to a river. A leaf falling slowly to the ground and landing without a sound on the soft grass. A flower petal. Not only do these images convey tenderness and peace to me, but they speak to me the simplicity of God's intent. He wants to enjoy and nurture His creation. Again, it's about relationships. Him and us. Us with others. What are the building blocks of healthy relationships? I believe they are the fruit of the Spirit. Gentleness is a heart disposition that overlaps with peace, self-control, and kindness. A gentle heart communicates peaceableness and maintains self-control. A gentle countenance extends kindness. As we are called to shepherd our children, let's ask the Holy Spirit to help us transmit these divine virtues filling us anew every day.

It's about relationships. Him and us. Us with others.

Years ago, I arrived early at a restaurant to meet my husband for lunch, and while I waited, I overheard a conversation that I'll never forget. A dad and his daughter sat in a booth across from me. I was trying not to listen, but every once in a while, I caught fragments of their conversation. Apparently, this dad was having an honest and vulnerable conversation with his preteen. Maybe a divorce or separation had occurred. Or perhaps there had been an early morning argument. I don't know, but the daughter was given permission to share her feelings. I glanced at the dad's face, and he was not offended but looking intently. Then I heard him say something like, "I struggle with that too."

...the daughter was given permission to share her feelings.

This dad reflected Jesus to his daughter. Jesus, our gentle Shepherd, walked inside of the human experience to be able to understand us—our struggle and our need. He was acquainted with grief and He carried our sorrow. He bore our sin which means He felt—internalized the struggle of sin and weakness. I'll never forget that dad. He was not perfect, but he humbly and kindly, gently and lovingly, related to his child. Oh, the beauty of bonding! When hearts share their weaknesses, the impenetrable bond of love is discovered.

Let gentleness be seen in every relationship, for our Lord is ever near.
Philippians 4:5, TPT

Being Gentle Doesn't Mean Being Weak

Proverbs 15:1 says that a soft answer turns away wrath. The Bible teaches that gentleness has the power to subdue anger. Often we think of gentle as being weak and fragile, but God's word gives us a different explanation. If gently answering a belligerent person takes the force out of their demeanor and behavior, then gentleness has the power of a weapon. This idea of greeting anger with a gentle response is supported in several places in the Bible. Corinthians 2:12 contrasts the spirit of the world with the Holy Spirit. Luke 6:28 tells us to bless those who curse us. Responding in anger to an angry person does not benefit anyone.

The Lord gave me a picture of how anger works. There was a day where I could feel it simmering inside and I didn't know why. I prayed. Nothing happened. So I just decided to dissect it by sensing what the anger was doing inside my soul. I wanted to learn more about how it was working. As I sat in a chair, I realized that anger felt like fire in an enclosed room. It wants to escape and find more oxygen to feed on. It desires to expand.

Think back to a time when you were angry. If you didn't deal with it quickly, how long did it take for you to start feeling resentful? Critical? Bitter? The problem with fire is that it must be fed or be stoked to survive. Have you ever heard of a backdraft? When a door opens, releasing oxygen into the fiery space, an explosion happens. Now it made sense why I, or anyone, had a hard time with self-restraint when feeling angry. The anger we feel tempts us to "open a door" or "vent". We yell, give the silent treatment, or do something in between, but when we are angry we let the energy of anger dictate our decisions and behavior.

But what puts out a fire? Water. The Holy Spirit is known as the living water (John 4:10) of God. Gentleness, a fruit of the Holy Spirit, is an anger quencher. When I got up from the chair after reflecting and "soul digging" for a while, my anger was gone. The Holy Spirit helped me find the trigger—an old unprocessed soul wound of not feeling loved. Having Him uncover the deep, ancient hurt was healing. It's like He said, "See, you are angry because you don't feel loved by people who said that they would love you. Sometimes they have been unloving and it hurts." Acknowledgment is a wonderful springboard to closure. For a few minutes, I let Jesus weep with the part of me that needed to shed deferred tears, and I forgave. I rebuked any evil that would try to send a fiery dart to hinder my healing. (Eph 6:16) Lastly, I realized that my fruit of

For a few minutes, I let Jesus weep with the part of me that needed to shed deferred tears, and I forgave.

self-control was more mature than it had ever been. I had successfully restrained myself from doing something petty to get back at the object of my anger (like take the last brownie that I knew they wanted), but I didn't. Instead of stoking anger by listening to the thoughts ruminating in my head, I sat in a chair and sought the gentle Shepherd. Spending time in quiet prayer—letting His Spirit dig up hidden hurts and His soft answers resolve our anger—leads to relief and growth.

In addition to having the power to neutralize anger—gentleness has the power to protect. Galatians 1:1 admonishes us to restore the broken, the offensive, the addict, and the weak with a spirit of gentleness. The verse reminds us that we can be overtaken in any weakness as they were. When counseling our kids or speaking truth to our spouses, a gentle spirit protects us from the sin of pride. In addition, gentleness protects those who need divine restoration and healing. Most of us know at least one person who has been hurt by authority figures or trusted believers who did not convey gentleness in their manner. This is such a sad reality. As parents, let's protect ourselves and our children by magnifying the importance of being gentle. When this virtue undergirds our manner, our children will be more willing to share and listen and we will stay humble.

Many of us have been victims. Whether our abuse was emotional, physical, or spiritual, we are repelled at the thought of being weak in the context of being taken advantage of. However, the more we understand what this virtue speaks about God, the more we'll know that walking in it will not put us in a precarious position. Gentleness is a manner that raises a person higher than their opponent. It resists the power of the enemy to make us respond in kind. As the redeemed, we are more than conquerors in Christ Jesus. Our spiritual position afforded to us

Gentleness is a manner that rises a person higher than their opponent.

by the work of Christ is one of authority. I will add that if you are in an abusive relationship, embracing gentleness does not mean that you should stay unsafe. Find a mature Christan or a resource that can provide you wisdom, emotional support, and physical safety if needed.

When the Storm Clouds Come

Becoming a parent immediately puts us in a position of risking being offended, hurt, and even forsaken. Situations will arise as suddenly as a summer storm with a fury that attempts to bruise the fruit we bear. Will we respond like our gentle Shepherd and use the power of gentleness to repair, reconcile and maintain relationships? No matter how many times your kids start yelling at each other or your teenager breaks curfew, pause and remember that the Spirit of God is with you and in you (Romans 8:11). If your teen does something serious, and the educational or legal systems get involved, the consequences can be serious. You will feel an array of emotions flood your soul, but ask God to make your first impulse the desire to respond in gentleness. Righteous anger is justified, yet a gentle response will diffuse the building tension. It will be a challenge, but it is possible to communicate our displeasure within a framework of gentleness. This means not flying off the handle, calling names, or reacting violently. We need to listen first, empathize with their shame, embarrassment, or fear of consequences, and then share our displeasure. Moreover, the front and back end of the conversation needs to communicate encouragement, vision for change, and forgiveness.

As stated before, this Spirit-led response—one based on the fruit of the Spirit and His divine prompting—will help put your child at ease, share more honestly, and possibly listen with humility. A gentle manner reduces defensiveness and limits the temptation for the offender to shut down. Ultimately, we want our teens to be able to admit any mistake or wrongdoing to us. We'd rather them tell us what happened before a police officer shows up at our doorstep. No matter how bad the storm is, we have to mirror the loving-kindness of God. Romans 2:4 reads, "...do you despise the riches of His goodness, forbearance, and longsuffering, not knowing that the goodness of God leads you to repentance?" Our gentle manner reflects God's goodness and forbearance. It's not easy. But just like us, our kids need to know they are valuable, accepted, and loved.

But the wisdom that is from above is first pure, then peaceable, gentle, willing to yield, full of mercy and good fruits, without partiality and without hypocrisy.
James 3:17

In this book, I focus on how our kids need to see us reflect God's response to them, but we also need to consider how we think the Lord responds to us. Like our kids, we do things that bring storms into our lives. We fail. We have bad attitudes. Our manner is harsh instead of gentle. But God's manner to us is gentle, kind, and forbearing. Does this surprise you? Do you stop praying after you commit sin or feel guilty for being tempted? It's tragic that many believers who stray from God's course and backslide often believe that God won't accept them back. We don't have to hide from God as Adam did. After a prodigal experience, we can come home to a father waiting expectantly and get a signet ring and a robe! Peter denied Jesus three times. Yet Jesus pursued Peter in his shame, not to accuse him or berate him, but to affirm and to reestablish him as His disciple. Despite the natural consequences of our bad choices, He forgives. Our gentle Shepherd is waiting to give us counsel and restore our fellowship

Despite the natural consequences of our bad choices, He forgives.

within the body of Christ. We must understand and walk in this if we are to model it to our children. Don't keep your distance from God when you have sinned.

It's all about relationships.

Prayer

Father, I thank You for walking with me every day. You are the Author and Finisher of my faith. You are the anchor of my soul, and I worship You. Lord, I confess that frustration and inconvenience often keep me from being gentle. At the same time, I recognize that gentleness is more than just an outward manner; it is a disposition of the heart that is anchored in forgiveness, mercy, and humility. Help me be slow to speak during those moments of difficulty. I recognize that I also need to be gentle with myself. Sometimes, I think harsh, unloving, and belittling thoughts about myself. Forgive me. Help me not only see others through Your eyes but help me see myself as You see me as well. In Jesus's name, Amen.

Quiet Time

Is gentleness one of the first attributes that comes to your mind when you think of God? Why or why not?

Gentleness requires humility. Confess any ways that your manner, words, or behavior have not reflected the humility of God. Choose 1-2 scripture verses from the chapter to memorize.

Chapter Seven

What is Good?

I found this definition in Easton's Bible Dictionary. Goodness "in man is not a mere passive quality, but the deliberate preference of right to wrong, the firm and persistent resistance of all moral evil, and the choosing and following of all moral good."

What a definition! Kind of "in your face" when it comes to the phrases "deliberate preference of right" and "firm and persistent resistance of all moral evil." The definition is like a magnifying glass to our willpower. Sometimes we are lazy and complacent when it comes to being attentive to our firmness in following Biblical morality.

My thoughts are not your thoughts,
nor are your ways my ways, says the Lord.
Isaiah 55:8

The Bible's standards are higher than those in our society. If we believe that God is good, then we'll obey His moral compass and not that of culture. We will acknowledge that a good God can only make good commands and guidelines. We'll accurately interpret Scripture as a whole and not live based on one story or one Scripture. For example, David had concubines, but God intends for married relationships to be monogamous. Abraham lied when he told Abimelech, the King of Gerar, that Sarah was his sister and not his wife (she was his half-sister but even half-truths are wrong), and all of them bore the consequence of his lie. Prioritizing what is right will be hard sometimes, but we must become convinced that honoring God's compass for what is "good" awakens our purpose and confirms our identity as sons and daughters of God.

Becoming Our Own Gods

Relativism is a paradigm of our post-modern world. Many people don't have God on their mental radar. Those in pop culture and the entertainment industry, many in political, and some even in educational circles. Moreover, many people believe that the concept of God is a human construct. If we don't stand firm in the personal revelation that we received by faith, we will be tempted to lean to our own understanding and go with the current tide. However, the God of the Bible is real. What if the tide is going away from His straight and narrow path? Not only must we remind ourselves of the reality of God's existence, based on Scripture and our deeply personal encounter that brought forth salvation, but we must also pause and consider God's perspective before we stroll into the shallow waters of human reasoning.

The soulish realm within us sometimes craves what we know is illegal, dangerous, or unhealthy. Nudged by the tempter, we reason as Eve did in the garden: "Oh, it couldn't be that bad" or "I need to decide for myself if this is dangerous." Unfortunately, advertisers do a great job of feeding upon these soulish cravings. While some things are blatantly and universally evil, like wanting to enslave others for personal benefit, what I will suggest is that most of our cravings come from legitimate longings that God gave us...but we set about satisfying them in ways that are sinful and harmful in the eyes of God.

This is a good place to remind us what the definition of sin is. Picture a bullseye. The center circle is the target for what God says is good, pure, and holy. Sin happens when we do not hit the target in our thoughts, manner, and actions. One further metaphor is that sin is an infection. It transmits through our blood. So every human being is infected. Understanding what sin is and how we were born with it can make living a holy life feel impossible. But Jesus broke the power and removed the infection for those who choose to believe in Him. As I've mentioned in previous chapters, our redemption paves the way to receiving God's enabling grace and empowering Spirit. When we remember what sin is, it does not make sense to ever lean to our own understanding. We need His reasons for why something is sin.

But even as Christian parents, we slip into thinking for ourselves, holding our opinions higher than what Scripture teaches, reasoning with the cultural tide and popular trends. Some of us let our kids decide for themselves what is good for them—what "good" means. But how is it ethically right to allow a child, whose cognitive and emotional capacity is still maturing, to define morality? Or gender? These are topics about which we have to allow the Spirit of God to guide us as we think on them. Part of this journey is renewing our minds according to God's moral compass, which can be found in His Word through faithful study.

Part of this journey is renewing our minds according to God's moral compass

As parents, we have to be honest about the degree to which we will lean to our own understanding because of our soulish cravings. Have you ever justified doing something based on your adult status? "We can handle it" is subtle reasoning that may cause us not to "acknowledge Him in all our ways" (Proverbs 3:6) We expose ourselves to things that we teach our children are wrong. It's genuinely hypocritical to expect more from our kids than we do for ourselves. We take the colors black and white and make them narrow but expand the array of hues of grey. In this vast "grey" zone, we become our own gods, doing what is right in our own sight instead of the sight of God.

In this vast "grey" zone, we become our own gods, doing what is right in our own sight instead of the sight of God.

There is only one God Most High. Let's put down our crowns and submit to what He says is good. For instance, ambition is a beautiful drive. It makes athletes excel, and a boy like my grandfather grow up to be a pathologist and brigadier general despite being raised by a single mother. This attribute doesn't settle for mediocrity. It's the war cry of a person who seeks to achieve the fullest possibility of who they can be. Philippians 2:3 warns against the perversion of ambition.

Let nothing be done through selfish ambition or conceit, but in lowliness of mind let each esteem others better than himself.

This verse says that we need to look out for not only our interests but the interests of others. Selfish ambition feeds a person's ego. It elevates our desires above the desires of other people. Selfish ambition disables us from being generous and compassionate. I think of a movie character that does whatever she can, walks over anyone in her way to get where she wants. The deception of selfish ambition is that it sucks the life out of the person. While the person thinks that they are living 'high on the hog,' they really have no life at all.

Take a minute and ponder how the fruit of goodness can ripen in your life. Share your thoughts with your children. What they hear you share and see you do will make an impression on them.

Our society has gotten divisive. Speak well of others instead of speaking your complaints or criticisms. Politics, a shifting moral landscape, and racial tensions can make us vent and be careless with our words. However, we can honor another person's humanity yet still disagree with their choices and beliefs. Since our kids need to witness us resisting moral evil, and adhering to moral good, our words about others should be respectful.

Another way to model Philippians 2:3 is through service. Involve your kids in the process of developing good character. Perhaps volunteer as a family at a local soup kitchen one weekend. One Saturday morning, we volunteered at a non-profit organization that takes meals to home-bound residents. The kids made Fall wreaths, pulled weeds, and cleaned out the refrigerated bags. They learned why people need to be cared for. The experience was a seed to make them think about the welfare of others. After this opportunity, I decided to volunteer to be a permanent driver on one route. Why keep my extra time to myself? I look forward to taking my kids with me on the route when they don't have school.

Find ways to bless your neighbors. Baked items and cards during the holidays are natural opportunities. Check on an elderly neighbor from time to time. When it comes to your professional goals, access who else will benefit from these goals besides yourself. How can you extend the gifts and blessings that God has given you to others? You may have to make some tough decisions. Unnecessary spending may lessen. We have to be deliberate in keeping our soulish desires and intents in line with God's moral compass.

Help your child understand that not everything is beneficial for them in the eyes of God. This may require you to vet movies and video games before your kids partake. You may decide not to upgrade your teenager's iPhone until you train them better on how to deal with their soulish cravings. As a family, you all can journey together to pursue moral goodness.

"But Everyone is Doing it!"

Raise your hand if you loved adolescence. I bet if I could see through my laptop, I would not see any hands raised. The teenage years are challenging, and the way our world is wired doesn't help. Contemporary culture for the teenager is a landfill of pop entertainment, verbal, fashion and hair trends, the latest social media interaction, entitlement, and escapism. Our adolescents are caught up in the tension between their childish immaturity and a rapidly maturing body. Then there is the volley between autonomy and groupthink. Somewhere along the way, because we began to expect teens to be slaves to their hormones, we've lowered the bar for their normal behavior and acceptable conduct.

We often tell our kids not to live a life based on the excuse "but everyone else is doing it." But how often do we fall into the same trap? Excusing behavior or decisions in favor of cultural groupthink can undermine the biblical principles that we once said we'd live by. Do you remember the moment when you declared "God, I'll live for you! I'll give you my whole life!" Our passion was notable, but we had little to no understanding of what that would require. Truthfully, some of us compartmentalize our life and have only given God a few of those compartments. Learning to love well is learning how to say, no, and teach our children to do the same. How often do we tell ourselves "no" to a particular TV show or website? Setting limits and boundaries is healthy for all of us.

We often tell our kids not to live a life based on the excuse, "but everyone else is doing it." But how often do we fall into the same trap?

Sometimes we reach roadblocks on the journey of parenting when our teens misbehave and resist "choosing and following moral good." We council them. We pray. We discipline them. We fight to resist getting angry and harsh. Sometimes we fail.

Their defiance and resistance may not be a conscious desire to sin. Sometimes our kids are snared by the wounds of their past. They misbehave out of pain or unresolved hurt. Perhaps they are exhibiting a generational weakness that needs God's power to remedy. As we are on a journey toward emotional health and wholeness, so are they. Each of us must lean on Jesus to guide us through these times.

Soul Work Goes Deep

Once my children became young adults, I hoped that opportunities would become available for them to reconcile anything in their past that caused them to struggle. I didn't want them to carry the baggage of childhood rejection or adolescent confusion into their adulthood. It is difficult, but we can assist our children's emotional healing.

Conversations this past week with my adult children were hard. To hear the stories of fear and loneliness, unclear advice about relating to the opposite sex, as well as self-imposed isolation and emotional suppression, shocked and saddened me. I never knew. This may seem hard to believe since I was a home educator who was pretty much around her kids much of the time. How can a child be lonely in a house full of people?

Conversations this past week with my adult children were hard.

Physical proximity does not mean emotional intimacy. In our culture, many people bond via the internet and texting. Those on the other side cannot look into our eyes and see the reality of our souls. Similarly, an always closed bedroom door is a serious barrier. Another cultural challenge is our hectic lifestyles. We can be so busy! This is not good. I've learned that more often than not, we must take the time to knock on our kid's door and enter their world. We need to eat meals together. We need to talk—no, listen to them, expecting at first to be met with the phrase, 'I'm fine.' However, we must keep knocking and making ourselves available, not just to be cheerleaders at sporting events or ballet recitals, but to be shoulders to cry on and hands to pray with. Unfortunately, many of us did not get this as children and teens. We entered parenthood with handicaps and didn't even realize it.

Sometimes our children need to see us own up to our failings to them. Honesty is always good. A detailed apology can go a long way. They need to know that we know how our mistakes, accidental or conscious, hurt them. My dad did this once. He acknowledged how many of his words and actions during my childhood and teenage years were not good. His apology healed a hole in my heart.

I heard someone say that we can only do the best we can, and we must trust God to fill in the rest. This is the truth. We are not perfect. We need to be good to ourselves by receiving God's help, mercy, and forgiveness. He didn't withhold His best—His Son—from any sinner or for any sin. This is mercy. As believers, we can rest that He will gently and methodically steer our hearts and heal our souls.

I now believe that maturity has to do less with our numerical ages and more with our emotional health. The Holy Spirit helps us respond, instead of reacting. He helps us to admit when we are wrong. He reminds us not to play the blame game. He molds us to be teachable and thankful. He stays with us on this journey to learn how to love well. The goodness of God is displayed when, despite the wounds of the past, our lives are transformed into beauty. As we come to Him with our hurts, He holds us, cries with us, and breathes His gentle breath into our memories, imparting healing.

Good Times Good Memories

I held back my tears pretty well despite the emotion that was heavy in the car as I drove my oldest son back to college for his last semester. The eight of us had had such a good time those last four weeks. As a family, we'd learned to be more real with each other, letting our most authentic selves be known without apology. During one of his last nights, we shared our prayer requests, our dreams, and our challenges, and then we prayed together, which was the icing on the cake. This time lasted almost four hours! It was amazing.

But to you who fear My name, the Sun of Righteousness shall arise with healing in His wings; and you shall go out and grow fat like stall-fed calves.
Malachi 4:2

As the soul of a family gets healed because each of us is maturing emotionally, goodness is more readily displayed. We laugh and cry together. We see each other through glasses half-full instead of half-empty. We have fun with one another. Judgment and criticism are abated, and we experience the goodness of God despite our weaknesses. Here is a prayer for all of us.

Prayer

God, You are benevolent, kind, and compassionate. You desire to remove the darkness, the pain, every aberration of Your intent from our lives so that goodness can flow through us. Lord, you are Jehovah-Rapha, God, our Healer. Heal the minds and emotions of my children so that they can move forward into the next stages of their lives without hindrance. Remove unhealthy generational weaknesses. Block the enemy's desire to persuade us through cultural opinions of morality.

Comfort our aching hearts as we acknowledge our failures and mistakes over the years. You give laughter, which can heal the soul and smiles that beautify our countenance. Even tears of joy are sweet to you! Remind us of your promise that healing, restoration, and satisfying life come to those who humble themselves before you. I love you, God, and I am thankful for your goodness.

Quiet Time

Healthy processing can still get heavy at times. Spend time singing your favorite hymns or worship songs. Singing is good for the soul.

Tell the Lord what you are thankful for. You can write a list, compose a poem, or just tell Him in a time of reflection. Even if you are in a time of crisis, tell Him a few items that make you thankful.

Chapter Eight

†

Joy: A Secret Weapon

Sometimes life with our kids is just plain amusing. Here is one of those episodes:

Our five-year-old son was eating a cheese stick and wiped his hands on the couch. My husband, Doug, reminded him that he should be using a napkin. I, sitting in an adjacent room, asked him in that maternal, reminding tone where he really should be eating. We'd previously discussed that using the dining room table for snacks is better than the coffee table in front of the couch.

"Wherever I want." He muttered as he walked around the room.

Doug: "What?!"

I looked up from my laptop and asked my husband: "Did he say what I think he just said?"

Doug nodded.

I got up and called this son to me. "Son, the words you used, and the manner you used them is called defiant. It means that you think your way is better than our way. You are a good boy, so you don't want to give answers that are not good."

He shuffled around in front of me and kept eating.

Son: "What should I say?"

Me: "Tell me the right answer. You know what the right answer is."

Son: "What if I want to say the same thing?"

"That is not the right answer. I don't want you to play around right now. Now, where should you be eating?"

Doug: "Yes, this isn't funny. Stop playing and give your mom the right answer."

Son: "On the roof!"

I tried hard to keep from laughing. Honestly, my son's "on the roof" answer was hilarious to me. Kudos to his raw and witty honesty. It was an ingenious response for a child who is just not ready to relent. He knew he wasn't prepared to comply and he let us know it. Maybe I could have laughed, but with my very intelligent five-year-old, I want to nip this sprout of attitude in the bud. Every parent and caregiver has dealt with this startling production of the human will. It's the classic "I'm standing up on the inside" story. But after 28 years of parenting, I've learned not to take any single situation of simple childishness too seriously. Sometimes raising kids is amusing.

The fruit of the Spirit of God is love, joy, peace, longsuffering, kindness, goodness, faithfulness, gentleness, and self-control. Joy is the second fruit named. Joy and happiness are two different things. Happiness comes and goes. But if joy is a fruit of the Spirit, then God is saying that it is supposed to be a continual way of being for those that believe. So, how does God explain joy?

The Certainty of God's Victory

You've heard the phrase that "joy is fleeting." I don't believe real joy is fleeting. It is a divine attribute that God plants within us like a seed. Its roots reinforce our perspective of God's faithfulness through hard times. Remember the story of Paul and Silas? They didn't sing lamentations while chained to the jail walls. They sang praises! Then there is the advice in James 1:2-8, which reads, "Count it all joy, when you fall into various trials, knowing that the testing of your faith produces patience." I've finally realized that it doesn't mean that God sends us bad trials to grow us up, and it doesn't mean that He puts us through tests to prove our love for Him. It means that He knows the Earth is a warzone, where evil opposes good, where the enemy seeks to steal, kill, and destroy. He is with us, teaching us how to reign over sin and resist the enemy. As we go through life, we will face the consequences of this warfare and our own bad decisions. But each challenge develops our faith—the ability to see the unseen but evident victory. One victory is our maturity. Therefore, despite the obstacles, we endure through life with joy because, in the end, we are more like Christ. Considering just these few verses, we see that joy has the power to undergird us in difficult times.

He knows the Earth is a warzone, where evil opposes good, where the enemy seeks to steal, kill, and destroy. He is with us...

The joy of the Lord is your strength.
Nehemiah 8:10

Consider it joy, my brothers and sisters when you face trials of many kinds
James 1:2-3

Joy involves strength and perspective. It has the power to hold us up in tough times. We think of the word strength primarily as muscular health and physical prowess; however, it also is mental resolve and emotional fortitude. This type of strength comes as we mature in Christ. As we prod through every challenge that our journey brings, we mentally resolve to focus on the faithfulness of God. In times of temptation, we bring our physical and emotional weaknesses to Jesus and let Him help us maintain healthy boundaries and godly safety. The joy of the Lord has the strength to help us endure and remain focused on Him.

Proverbs 15 reminds me of the process of doing a puzzle. We see two pieces that look like the right fit but are not. But when we find the exact one that fits, we exclaim, "I've found the right piece!" A state of rightness occurs. It's just "right." Have you ever said to someone, "That was just what I needed to hear!" When we give a timely or appropriate response to someone, joy is produced in them. The word strengthens them.

A man has joy by the answer of his mouth, and a word spoken in due season, how good it is!
Proverbs 15:23

Joy can produce emotion, but it is not an emotion. Sometimes we read James 1 and think that we need to jump for joy when our child gets pulled into the principal's office. We don't have to be happy, but we can have joy, which undergirds our perspective on the outcome of our child's experience.

Celebrate Victories Big and Small

Another verse that talks about joy is Psalm 30:5: *"Weeping may endure for a night, but joy comes in the morning."* Parenting can make us weary and frustrated. Do you have a child that for whatever reason deals with procrastination? I once did. As a task-oriented person, reminding him—nagging him—would wear me out. I prayed and prayed and encouraged, and yes, nagged some more. All I could think about was how poorly they would do in college if they didn't get their act together now! The Holy Spirit used Psalm 30:5 to encourage me. He also reminded me that my child's time management skills would develop one day. To wait with joy, I had to change my focus. One idea to alleviate my weariness was to celebrate any small victory, like when he accomplished a goal that he'd set for himself.

Have you ever glossed over a moment when your child finally "gets it?" Did your attitude express: "They are finally doing what they are supposed to!" Can you hear the tone in those words? I've been guilty of this as well. It's as if our kids are doing us a favor to comply, that it took too long, and it deserves no recognition because it's expected behavior. Instead of my self-righteous and ungrateful mindset, I need to stop and take in the moment. "Honey, what a great decision to begin to do your homework right now! Good job!"

We can give our child a high-five or a fist-bump. Let's celebrate our children's victories, big and small, by making a mental note that seeds do germinate in time. Etch those moments in our memory banks so that just in case the same wise decision isn't made the next day, we can know that our training is slowly working. We have to stay encouraged and let joy be a weapon that cuts off discouragement.

The details of managing a household are like the giants that the Israelites faced when they saw the promised land. They are constant, and they are overwhelming! Our tension builds. Because of our responsibilities and the messiness of family life, we begin to react instead of respond. Diapers, lunches, whines, spills, missing homework, medical appointments, work, meetings, oil changes, sibling rivalry, unexpected data charges, mood swings, marital spats, pimples, laundry, college applications, uniforms—whew! Life overwhelms us and makes us feel like grasshoppers (Numbers 13:33).

Let's expect that giants will always exist. Every age and stage of our child's life will bring issues that overwhelm us. We can grumble and complain, or we can realize that no matter how much we pray heaven into our homes, perfection is not for our earthly life. When we expect that our kids are sometimes going to throw tantrums and give us a lousy attitude, joy can offset the tension that builds in us. Today on the way to church, my 8-year-old asked me why I hadn't told him about an event that he wouldn't be able to attend. I responded, "Because I didn't want to hear you complain and ask me 200 questions about why you couldn't go." He paused and said, "You're smart." I smiled, looked in the rearview mirror and said, "I know." He smiled back. It's nice for both parent and child to be able to find these potentially aggravating moments joyously amusing.

Musicians and athletes understand that repetition builds muscle memory. This is why being thankful and celebrating the things we often take for granted—like having a place to live, is so important. Switching our focus from negativity to a positive outlook takes effort and practice. The human will is like a muscle. We have to work to keep our joy from being quenched. When we are intentional about thinking on things that are lovely, true, worthy of praise, etc. it will be easier to have a joyful heart. But like developing muscle memory, it takes repetition and effort. As we practice being thankful and finding at least one thing to celebrate each day, we will find that joy doesn't slip away easily but remains our necessary undergirding of strength.

When we are intentional about thinking on things that are lovely, true, worthy of praise, etc. it will be easier to have a joyful heart.

Embracing Spontaneous Moments

Jesus' first miracle was amid a joyous occasion. He and his mom were invited to this festive Hebrew celebration. Music played, and the dancing was constant. The wine was flowing too, so much that the host ran out of it. A quick aside—God always warned the

Israelites about drunkenness. I'd like to think that they ran out of wine not because they were all drunkards, but that there were so many people in attendance. Who knows? Regardless, Jesus turned barrels of water into the tastiest wine. Created in an instant, it must have tasted as if it had aged for decades.

Jesus' first miracle wasn't raising someone from the dead or healing a person who had been sick for months. No, His first miracle was done in an atmosphere of joy. I believe this speaks powerfully to God's opinion of pleasure, fun, and celebration.

And a time to laugh;
A time to mourn,
And a time to dance;
Ecclesiastes 3:4

Seeds grow and bear fruit when the ground is healthy. We should often remind ourselves that as we pursue spiritual and emotional wholeness, the atmosphere of our homes will be as good ground.

You will show me the path of life; In Your presence is fullness of joy; At Your right hand are pleasures forevermore.
Psalm 16:11

Ever have some music on and just start dancing in the middle of the floor? I'm talking about that silly goofy dancing. I do this at times and try to coax any of my six kids to participate. Usually, it's just the youngest ones and lasts only for a few minutes. It's fun to create fun. Spontaneous love-filled fun. We've got to unclutter our schedules to allow for such spontaneity and joy.

When laughter erupts spontaneously in your house, there is joy. When playfulness happens even though you fought with your spouse the night before, it is a sign that joy is a part of the foundation of your home. It means there is security. Everyone knows that they belong and are accepted. No one fears not being liked or unwanted. I love what King David wrote in Psalm 16:11. David found what all of us want: the fullness of joy and eternal pleasure, which is encapsulated in the life that God intends for us. In this scripture, a powerful truth is unveiled. Only in God's presence can we find both joy and pleasure.

This book is about how to put our families in a position to prosper emotionally, spiritually, and relationally by focusing on our process of emotional maturity. The fruit of the Spirit is the outward manifestation of our reliance on the Holy Spirit and a result of maturing in Christ. Continual dependence allows Him to cultivate these virtues.

May the God of hope fill you with all joy and peace as you trust in him, so that you may overflow with hope by the power of the Holy Spirit...
Romans 15:13

Joy Will Come!

Have you ever been awake during the night, mind filled with fears, and your heart unsettled about issues with your kids? I have. During my quiet time one morning after a night like this, I reclined with a blanket and gazed back and forth from the shadows of dawn outside to the flames of the candles that I had lit. (I don't usually light candles when I pray; it was a spontaneous decision.) As I sat in the recliner, I was honest with the Lord about the season of my life. I also found a few scriptures to meditate on. Then as I stared into the flame, His still, soft voice reminded me, *My Light overcomes darkness.* What a timely, sweet moment this was! God took advantage of the flickering candles to give me the

As I sat in the recliner, I was honest with the Lord about the season of my life.

perspective that would bring me joy. I wonder if He looked down and decided, *Since she lit a candle, I will use that as a visual aid for her.* His reminder replaced fear with faith, tension with peace. His presence wasn't physically tangible, but my inner being responded to His comfort; ...it seemed as if His holy realm had come into the room. I relaxed and rejoiced Nothing in my circumstances had changed. But my perspective shifted because of His Word. Joy was rekindled in a moment.

It's easy to have joy when life is good. The paycheck is deposited. No one is sick. Jesus performs His first miracle at a wedding. He wants to celebrate good times with us. Good times are worth celebrating! Equally important is maintaining the fruit of joy when life is hard. It takes effort. But the benefit of this virtue is that it sustains us when our circumstances weigh us down. God's joy undergirds our emotions by keeping our perspective on His ability, His power, and His heart for us. God, our Creator can make water out of wine. This involves bringing change on a molecular level! Surely, He can bring triumph out of tragedy. Take a look at all of the verses in the Book of Psalms declaring that He is our refuge. His heart is for us. We don't have to worry about being without help because He sent us His Spirit to be our helper.

Prayer

Lord Jesus, I need Your joy to undergird my life. In each situation, give me the perspective needed to maintain joy. No matter what's going on, help me be thankful because You are with me and You are working things out. I want my kids to see me smile and hear me laugh. As a family, help us be emotionally honest—in good times and challenging times. In tough seasons, let the acknowledgment of Your faithfulness be the bookend to each day. Please help me make room in my life for spontaneity, whether it's spontaneous fun and laughter with my spouse, kids, and friends, or whether it is spending time in Your presence. In Jesus' name, Amen.

Quiet Time

Get your Bible and finish various scriptures about joy. Pick a couple to memorize.

Listen to what you say during the next few days during casual conversations. Listen to your responses to people. Do your words reveal any fear, criticism, or lack of gratitude? Find someone you trust to pray with you concerning these things.

Chapter Nine

†

The Necessity of Peace

A time to love,
And a time to hate;
A time of war,
And a time of peace
Ecclesiastes 3:8

2002. The exhilaration of homeschooling my kids had dissipated. My husband and I were doing full-time ministry on a part-time schedule. The bottom level of our townhouse was being renovated to add a needed bedroom, and the 9/11 attack was fresh in my mind. My outlook on life was grey.

As far as homeschooling, my kids weren't the problem. Teaching was not the issue. It was me. The noose of perfectionism was stealing my vitality and my peace. Each of us has something—a mindset, a person or a circumstance, that tries to steal our peace. But peace must be so valuable, so precious to us, that we take time to pinpoint what we need to do, how we need to think, in order to let the peace of God rule and reign in our hearts.

The Perfectionism and Striving

When had I adopted the picture of the multi-tasking, never sleeping, Betty Crocker housewife? Honestly, I have no idea. I loved everything that I did. Music, ministry, teaching, and even learning how to frame walls tapped into my childhood fantasy of being a carpenter. But doing anything is hard when you are trying to live up to a self-imposed image. My merciless inner overlord wanted to cry out, "I am woman, hear me roar!" Instead, most days, all I could muster was a feeble yelp.

My perfection based, fear of failure mindset was spoiling the fruit of peace. But God stepped in and gave me the revelation that peace is like a breath of fresh air, a gentle wind wafting through our lives. I craved it. I had to decide to fight for it.

Perfectionism withdrawal took a few years. Actually, almost a decade. Self-condemnation had to be rooted out as did pride and concern for the opinions of others. I learned that my school day could be flexible. The kids didn't have to follow a public school's schedule. I could give them a two-hour break in the afternoon and finish up in the evening or on a Saturday. As far as always being available to pray with or counsel someone in need, I had to learn to say, "I can't meet you this week" with no guilt.

Having a Mary Kay face each day became a distant memory. Good-bye "quick" beauty regimen; eyeliner and mascara could suffice. I still cooked each day because recipes fed my creative mind. As far as the post-9/11 soberness in the American air, I wondered if my children would grow up in a world where domestic peace was mythic.

Eventually, our days became more relaxed as I resisted the accusing demons. So what if every day I sat on the floor playing blocks with my three-year-old while rehearsing spelling words with my first grader as my elementary school kids read or did math? It didn't look like the traditional classroom, but it worked!

So what if a cup of milk spilled on the floor in the middle of a history lesson? I breathed easier once the noose of perfectionism was gone.

All of my six children have exhibited this cursed characteristic of perfectionism. Doug talked the other day with one of them about blocked goals. When our goals are unreasonable for ourselves and others, we get frustrated when they are not met. In this case, the child wanted an A+ in every class but had received a B and a B+ amid an array of A's. Doug appreciated that the child wanted all A's, but with Latin being a new subject, he knew that the child's lack of grace for themselves would end up being dangerous to his emotional wellbeing. Striving to have perfect grades, a perfectly clean house, a perfect nighttime routine can be helpful, but when things don't go our way, this idealism and perfectionism will steal our peace.

No matter what type of labor we do, what kind of goals we make, we must try not to strive to maintain a self-imposed or worldly standard that makes us driven, harsh, worried, or stressed out. I know that there are professional environments that are "dog-eat-dog," but we can ask ourselves, "Are the pressures worth my peace, which is a precious commodity for my soul? What about my health and joy? Are the pressures of my job worth losing those things?"

Peace has value. It boosts our immune systems and helps us sleep at night. Many of us live in a mode where a level of anxiety and an unhealthy level of stress is normal. We've become comfortable with frenetic micromanaging and full daily schedules. We all need to ask ourselves, "What are we trying to prove and to whom?" If we are doing whatever the Lord has put on our agendas, He will help us with those tasks. We don't have to fear not accomplishing what He has for us. Sometimes, if we pause to look under the surface of our motives, we'll find a soul

"What are we trying to prove and to whom?"

issue or two. Maybe we can't say no—we fear disappointing people. Or perhaps we are lonely and activity fills the void. We have to believe that the Prince of Peace wants His people to have peace and be willing to change our lifestyle if needed.

Don't Focus on Your Lack

In the past two weeks, I've been struck by the mother in 1 Kings 17. Her courage to believe God's word changed the outcome of her circumstances. More so, she had an air of uncanny peace.

To summarize the story: the widow was getting wood to prepare one last meal for herself and her son when Elijah shows up on the scene. Elijah, a well-known prophet, wants some food. She lets him know that they don't have enough food to share with him. At that time, it's remarkable that they had food at all because the land was experiencing a famine, and she was a widow. We don't know how long her husband had been dead. She was probably younger than thirty because the Bible calls her son "a child" later in the passage. Economically, this impoverished single mother had no hope during this drought. Circumstances beyond her control had taken over her life. Then she hears the words: "Feed me first, and God will continue to provide for you until it starts raining again."

How many of you would listen to some stranger rolling up on your doorstep saying the same thing? That would tick me off. Gentle words would not be rolling off my tongue! Verse nine reveals that Elijah met the widow, knowing that God had already commanded her to feed him. He was a man of faith. If God told him to do something, he knew God was going to move.

Her natural eyes saw a lack in her home. She and her son heard each other's hunger pangs. But we see her do what Elijah asks. She fed him first. As a mother, she'd probably been making her son's last meal cakes a tad bit larger than hers even though she knew that death was inevitable for them both. Her visible reality shouted, "Death!" But in another human being's words, she heard the voice of God. She trusted that God was speaking to her through another human being. She heard Elijah's words and did what he said. Wow! God was the source of this Old Testament single mother's peace.

Maintaining inner peace becomes more complicated when a spouse isn't in the picture or works multiple jobs as my husband did in our early years of marriage. Being the only parent around is tough. I've never been a single parent, and I can't imagine carrying the responsibilities for raising kids and running a household, as well as being the sole provider. When Doug worked 90 hours per week, and I didn't see another adult for days on end, it was tough to keep finding peace in my current situation. I loved motherhood, but I didn't like the long hours. I was still getting up to nurse a baby or soothe a toddler who had just woken up from a bad dream. Then it hit me. Jesus could sleep peacefully in a storm! His disciples had to wake him up! I needed greater confidence in my Father's care. Although I felt alone, I wasn't. He was in the boat with me. I had to believe that God had purposed to get me to the other side of that season.

Sometimes what displaces peace is the fear that our situation is hopeless.

Sometimes what displaces peace is the fear that our situation is hopeless. We can't see the other side of a challenge, and we let our thoughts drift away from what His word says about our future. *For I know the thoughts that I think toward you, says the Lord, thoughts of peace and not of evil, to give you a future and a hope* (Jeremiah 29:11), Holding onto these truths will help us stay in a place of incomprehensible peace.

He is the anchor of our soul (Hebrews 6:19); therefore, we won't fall apart, even when we feel emotionally drained.

He will never leave us nor forsake us (Hebrews 13:5); therefore, we know He is there to help us fight our battles.

He turns our mourning into dancing (Psalm 30:11). Every season is temporary. He gives us endurance when life is tough.

Heaven contains the throne of peace. Desiring and praying for "on earth as it is in heaven" teases our longing because we know that indeed earth will never be heaven, and heaven is the ideal that we desire. Despite that, the peace of Jesus Christ (James 14:27), secures us to a foundation when everything else around us is unsteady. It comes when we fix our eyes on our God who cannot change.

Seasons of Change

Circumstances change all the time. Jobs, finances, people—all of us experience unwelcome change. But we want security. In fact, we need security. However, if we make these things the source—the provider of our peace—then we are going to be in turmoil if something ever happens to them.

Change is troublesome and meddles with our sense of security and comfort. When our world one day is vastly different from the day before, we experience various levels of stress. Those of you who remember 9-11 know what I mean. Our minds reel when life as we knew it, can never be recovered. Once, I asked myself, "How comfortable am I supposed to be on this side of heaven?" The challenge of our earthly life is to wait for what we know will come but cannot be at present: consistency, constant safety, and social unity. Times of laughter, rest, and fulfillment do give us a glimpse

When our world one day is vastly different from the day before, we experience various levels of stress.

of eternity with God, but our daily reality involves difficulty and change and stress stifles our peace.

I've learned that once the first child leaves home or goes to college, that family life is a constant transition period. All members, even younger siblings, have to adjust to a new norm. It's not always easy. Several months after my dad died, one of my kids moved across the country, and soon after that, my fourth child left for college. Despite the quieter evenings—due to fewer people going in and out, peace had left the premises. Our hearts were in agony. Mourning. Our minds reeled. Not only had my heart experienced emotional whiplash, but the revolving door of change was affecting my youngest kids. I knew they were misbehaving because of the pain of their loss.

Even though hard seasons seem to last forever, they are momentary. As we trudge through them, God wants us to remember that peace comes from the fact that He never leaves us. He is unchanging and must be our constant source of peace. He alone provides the safety of His unchanging nature and abiding presence. Through times of change, He squeezes our hands to let us know that He's holding on tight and won't let us go. Even though sometimes we cannot tell that He is close, He is.

Through times of change, He squeezes our hands to let us know that He's holding on tight and won't let go.

Finding the Peace of God

If you are like me, sometimes you feel like you are drowning. To keep afloat, I take advantage of the moments when God's peace is tangible. Like when I walk through the woods on a crisp spring or fall morning. The air during these seasons is invigorating and fresh, unlike the heavy blanket of our humid southern summer mornings. Our summer beach vacations are my favorite time of year. Gazing out into the ocean and listening to the waves puts me in a place of stillness. I embrace these holy pauses in life and stroll the shores knowing that God is smiling down on me. The colder winter months are more difficult for me because I yearn for the soft sand, caressing breezes, and seemingly endless time of summer vacations. But it's nice to sit on the deck and watch the flames dancing in the fire pit. While nature often reflects the wildness of our lives, it is one place where I sense His peace-filled presence. I wrote this poem on a beautiful sky-blue day after an evening stroll.

Wafting across my body,
Peace makes me lay still.
Every atom in sync with holy vibrations
Dissonance floats away with the breeze.
I see my hand
Extend beyond my Self
Fingers outstretched to grab
The Unseen.
If I could only peel off this mortal flesh
The eternal me could inhale,
Fill my lungs to overflowing
Then be buoyed into the wind.
I'd soar. I'd roam.
I'd be tossed.
Thank you flesh
For chaining me to earthly limitations.
Though I yearn for Heaven. (T. Webb 2017)

Do you have a special place that calls out to you? When you finally get there, you become still. Aware. And your mind naturally begins to think about God. Buried prayers come from your heart. Times of prayer is usually where God fills my soul with peace. I take advantage of the times when no one is home. I sit, close my eyes, and in my heart, I ask the Holy Spirit to calm me from my frenetic to-do lists and weekly planning. When that precious time is over, it's hard to want to resume my day. There is an earthly tension that can become our norm, but we must take time, even contend for time, where we can find a quiet space to allow Christ's peace to fill our hearts.

A Mission of Peace

Peace in these days seems conceptual and otherworldly. Certainly not realistic. Where on our globe does peace exist right now? The deluge of controversy and relational tension can be stressful. Turmoil is displayed before our eyes on the news and social media. Many kids are caught up in the negativity as well. In the past month, I've read two articles about the effects of social media on children and teens. Online bullying? Yes. The fact that our young are committing suicide at increasing rates is troublesome. Bullying, the fear of rejection, or the general atmosphere of chaos is more than tragic for our kids. They need peace. But how do we as parents give them peace when even we are contending for it?

One of my favorite songs as a child was "Let There Be Peace on Earth." Songwriters Jill Jackson and Sy Miller captured in words and melody the longing of every human heart for peace. I must have been a third-grader in Shaker Heights, Ohio when I first heard the song during music class. I absolutely loved it. My soul latched onto its inspiration so much that those lyrics still flow from my memory banks forty years after learning it.

God's heart isn't callous toward the lack of peace on earth. Isaiah 9:7 suggests that ever since Jesus came, God's government and His peace is increasing! Jesus left us His own peace because He knew that the world's version of peace would not suffice to meet our innate longing for constancy and security.

Peace I leave with you, My peace I give to you; not as the world gives do I give to you.
John 14:27

What exactly does Jesus' version of peace look like? As I peruse the Bible, two Scriptures stand out. One deals with Jesus' purpose and the other, the focus of His gaze. Jesus said in John 4:34, this sobering statement. *"My food is to do the will of Him who sent Me, and to finish His work."* Jesus clearly states that the purpose of His earthly existence was to fulfill God's intentions and finish the Father's work. This verse references God's will to restore mankind to Him. It is not God's will that anyone should perish—be eternally separated from Him. 2 Peter 3:9 is clear about this and also that He wants every human being to repent and be saved. He is a rescuer, restorer, and redeemer. Jesus' second phrase speaks of his role in completing God's work. What work had God already begun? After Adam and Eve sinned, there was a veil—a separation between them and their Creator. Instead of peace on earth, sin brought a new level of chaos. Human beings were at odds with one another. We see God begin the work of reconciliation, or I could say, restoring His original intent, when He first spoke to Abraham. I believe that the intentional dissemination of Jesus' peace in John 14:27 is a part of the finishing work of the Father. Jesus was sent from heaven on a mission of reconciliation. This fed Him. What a powerful metaphor! Just as food nourishes our physical bodies, His mission of reconciliation—bringing peace between enemies (Colossians 1:21) nourished Him. Jesus gave us His peace so that we could be peacemakers. It is our God-given mission to be reconcilers. Carriers of the gospel of peace, who through His power, bring peace between opposing factions.

> His mission of reconciliation – bringing peace between enemies, nourished Him.

The other instance that tells me about Jesus' version of peace is John 17:1-5. This passage is loaded, but what I want to point out is Jesus' reliance on the Father that came through the certainty of their relationship. It set His countenance and perspective when it came to the mission. Jesus, the incarnate Christ, put aside His divine privileges to live as a human being to understand our plight, bear our sin, and satisfy our longing to be reconciled with our Creator.

Jesus spoke these words, lifted up His eyes to heaven, and said: "Father, the hour has come. Glorify Your Son, that Your Son also may glorify You, as You have given Him authority over all flesh, that He should give eternal life to as many as You have given Him. And this is eternal life, that they may know You, the only true God, and Jesus Christ whom You have sent. I have glorified You on the earth. I have finished the work which You have given Me to do. And now, O Father, glorify Me together with Yourself, with the glory which I had with You before the world was.

John 17:1-5

Jesus finished His work. He pointed human beings—you and me—enemies of God through sin, to the Father, our Creator. He left us His peace to use to carry on His mission. His peace is one of certainty and security with the Father. So as believers, we have that too. Certainty and security in our relationship with the Father.

Jesus lived in a jaw-dropping state of peace despite being hated and rejected by many and despite living under oppressive Roman rule. He was not moved by circumstances; rather, He moved circumstances. He slept during a storm when veteran fishermen were freaking out. To stay peaceful, Jesus did not look at His circumstances. Neither should we. Furthermore, Jesus often got away. He went to the top of the mountains to have quiet time and pray. Each of us needs to find that spot and time of day that we can get recharged through spending time with God. I am certain that Jesus' version of peace had to do with His relationship with the Father. Through Him, the Prince of Peace, we now have a relationship with the Father. And He does not change! The one constant we have, as believers, is our unchanging God. Friendships change and kids grow up. The world changes. But our peace on earth is linked to our relationship to the Father, the One who desired our existence and sent Jesus to restore us to Him.

Prayer

Lord Jesus, I read that peace can guard my heart and my mind. (Philippians 4:7) You also say that You'll give me Your peace—not the peace of the world. (John 14:27) I receive Your version of peace. Without it, I can't sleep. I experience so much confusion and disarray, I need Your peace to guard my soul.
As every year goes by, as the ages and stages of my kids change, as my relationships go through ups and downs, I need You as the anchor of my soul…my emotions, my will, and my thoughts. Anchor me in Your love. Remove any doubt in me and show me that you are faithful. You are constant, and in this, I can rest and be secure. You are the Prince of Peace. Spirit of God fill me now to overflowing. Give me the peace that surpasses my understanding.

Quiet Time

In the next 48 hours, try to schedule some time where you can be alone. It can be outside, at home, or even in your car. Take that time to be silent.

What was the hardest season of change in your life? Consider writing down words or phrases that described what it was like. Ask God to reveal if that moment of change still affects you?

Is there a relationship in your life that brings stress or tension? Ask Jesus to bring peace between you and the person. This may include taking time to acknowledge the array of emotions you feel, forgiving, and praying for the person with a humble heart.

Chapter Ten

†

Loving Through the Wounds

"I hate you."

Those words don't sting as they once did. However, the first time I heard that phrase from someone that I loved deeply, it was a dagger, despite the mask that I wore for their benefit. I knew they didn't mean it. It had been a bad two weeks for them, and their emotional turmoil was affecting a few of their relationships, including ours. I'd permitted this person to be honest, and this was their answer. It would have been hypocritical for me to say, "Please, be honest about how you are feeling right now. I want you to be able to say anything at this moment," and then exhibit shock and anger when they took me up on my invitation. So I wore a mask for them. Later, I let Jesus tend to my heart and the incidents that may have led up to them feeling that way toward me. About a month later, they recanted, as I knew they would. The Scripture that I held on to was:

"Do the riches of his extraordinary kindness make you take him for granted and despise him? Haven't you experienced how kind and understanding he has been to you? Don't mistake his

tolerance for acceptance. Do you realize that all the wealth of his extravagant kindness is meant to melt your heart and lead you into repentance?
Romans 2:4 TPT

To mirror our heavenly Father to this loved one, I had to put on my big-girl pants, acknowledge the season of emotional disarray that they were in, and extend kindness to them.

While this demonstration of kindness can be difficult to display, it is a form of beneficence and altruism. Kindness, from the Hebrew word, *checed or hesed,* is sometimes translated as lovingkindness. This word involves extending warmth toward everyone around us. It has the power to uplift and makes someone feel wanted. Kindness considers someone regardless of circumstance and extends benefits whether they deserve it or not. Therefore, this virtue involves mercy—part of the nature of God that humbles us. We don't deserve God's kindness, but we get it. The ultimate extension of His kindness was His Son, who took our sins and gave us His righteousness. I call this the great exchange. Once we understood what He was offering: grace, redemption, and unconditional love, our only natural response was to change our mindsets, surrender our will, change direction, and follow His ways.

Pushing Through Pain

I recall too many incidents when someone intentionally or unintentionally cut me down with their words or the tone of their words. You may also remember an experience when your child spoke to you rudely, or your spouse made a snide remark. Don't you remember how, as soon as their words hit your ears, your blood began to run cold? Or you felt like you'd been punched in the gut? Words have weight. The Scripture teaches us that our words have both the power to burn relationships and the power to bring forth a sense of worth. Harmful words light a flame of destruction both between people and within people's souls. I've prayed with so many people that have struggled as adults because of the verbal wounds they suffered when they were young. Scripture says that the tongue is a source of destruction.

And the tongue is a fire, a world of iniquity…sets on fire the course of nature; and it is set on fire by hell.
James 3: 6

Death and life are in the power of the tongue, and those who love it will eat its fruit.
Proverbs 18:21

Sometimes we incorrectly believe that we need to point out someone's faults to show them how much they have wronged us. Certainly, there are times when we must go to an offender, not to make them feel our pain, but to bring the understanding needed to restore the harmony of the relationship. The manner makes all the difference. Kindness does not allow a negative incident to skew or change our interaction with someone else. I am often convicted of my reaction when one of my children back talks or speaks rudely to me. It is my duty to help them understand the effects of their words, but in doing so, I cannot blow up at them. If I am to reflect Jesus, then the intent of my heart must be to let them know that I love them anyway. My kindness towards them or anyone cannot be condition-based.

God gives us all the right to feel, to emote, and to process. Romans 12:15 says to weep with those who weep. Jesus did. There was mourning in the air when he arrived at the tomb of Lazarus. To be emotionally healthy, we must be emotionally present. If someone hurts me, on purpose or by mistake, as soon as I can, I get alone with Jesus. Jesus acknowledges our sadness; our hurt. He weeps with us. The willful decision to forgive does not always cancel hurt emotions in the soul. While our will and our emotions are interconnected, they are also two different components.

There are times in parenting, marriage, or just friendship when our love seems to dissipate, or we just don't "like" that son, spouse, or friend at the moment. Our emotions are numb. It is easy to give a cold shoulder when someone hurts our feelings. Sometimes, in our hurt, we wear our negative emotions like a cross that we must bear for a time. What do we do when we feel so cold inside because someone has brutally wrecked our confidence in them? Kindness in these times is a sacrifice. We acknowledge our emotionally cold inner world, but we make an effort to be amicable with that person. While doing this, we keep our hearts open to the supernatural touch of the Holy Spirit. These verses offer a very inhuman result of the power of kindness. Kindness promotes change in the offender and makes our hearts feel warm again.

...do you think lightly of the riches of His kindness and tolerance and patience, not knowing that the kindness of God leads you to repentance?
Romans 2:3-4

Kindness doesn't erase the offense, but it acknowledges the offender as a fellow human being made in the image of God, worthy of acceptance despite their infraction. Over time, God heals our wound, comforts our sorrow, and strengthens our ability to be like Him and extend kindness no matter what. Kindness is kin to forgiveness. It gives what the offender does not deserve. Forgiveness does not erase the memory—doesn't even end emotional pain—but it relieves the person from our desire to avenge ourselves. The process of healing requires us to embrace our anger and sadness but choose to put our offense on the cross of Christ, who bore their sin as He did our own.

Once we forgive, the power of kindness operates in full tilt. If the offender continues in their negative behaviors, no matter what protective boundaries are given, continue to be kind but involve others to bring support and insight.

Kindness Makes a Difference

Modeling spontaneous moments of kindness is a great way to impart this virtue to our kids. I began by keeping packs of granola bars and water bottles in my van. If I stopped at a traffic light and a homeless person was there with a sign, we'd have something to offer. I do give dollar bills when I have cash on hand. My younger kids are so used to this random act of kindness that when we slow down at a light, and they see someone with a sign, they ask, "Mom, do you have a couple of dollars?"

Once Doug and our older kids were leaving the movie theatre when they saw a man fall on an icy sidewalk. Doug turned his SUV around and pulled to the side of the road. The man was older and ended up being fine. Since they were heading in one direction down a usually busy street, it would have been easy to keep driving and just say a prayer. But Doug modeled kindness to our kids. I'm sure there are many opportunities that we've missed or ignored. Kindness often involves inconvenience. We can dig to discover why we don't like to be inconvenienced. Often, it's because of self-centeredness, which is sin.

Kindness extends care and courtesy. Volunteering without being asked, smiling at a stranger, or thanking the janitor at your child's school are significant gestures of kindness. They extend warmth to the recipients and even make us feel good inside. After all, it's nice to be a blessing. At the same time, God teaches us selflessness. To put others before ourselves, no matter what. It's not always easy. On my website, I feature stories of people who are impacting the culture around them in very deliberate and Christlike ways. My August 2019 story was a scene that I had observed that displayed the power of kindness. Both a Black woman and a White man had a mind to be kind, despite a racial climate that could have produced a different decision.

> I was in the Chick-Fil-A drive-thru in Charlottesville, Virginia. A young Black woman walked in front of an elderly White man. She opened the door, but instead of entering first and holding the door open behind her, she paused to let him walk around her and enter first. Whether deferring to his age or because he was White, I'll never know. But he shook his head, reached for the door, and nodded for her to enter first. It impressed me. Unknowingly, his action could have contradicted some of her personal experiences. His response was "counter-culture" to what many believe about this place.
>
> (tinawebb.net/in-the-news/)

Today in America, we are experiencing increased relational dissonance. The disconnect between the generations, races, genders, and political parties is a dilemma that our unseen enemy is using to try to block the power of kindness. This division lies at our doorstep and tries to breed itself in our homes. At the root is sin. But this enemy, unseen and often ignored, steals, kills, and destroys wherever he can, from city street to dining room table. As believers, the extenders of the Kingdom of God, we are called to be on guard and to live in an opposite spirit, where loving-kindness defeats animosity.

This division lies at our doorstep and tries to breed itself in our homes.

As parents, we have to dissect our opinions and emotions to find anything that God is highlighting. Prejudice can be subtle for many of us. God can uncover seeds that we inherited from our ancestors or were imparted by our circles of influence. We can use current events to cultivate the souls of our children. When we explain a news report about sexism in the workplace to our kids, we can ask them their thoughts and what emotions come up. When accessing ourselves, we can learn from our manner—the words we speak and how we speak them. What do we say to our kids when they hear or use a racial slur, or have a different political point of view than someone they know? How we explain these issues to them is as important. Body language and tone reveal a lot about the seedbed of our souls. Every day, His Spirit is searching out any belief or opinion that would be a barrier to kindness.

Kind Discipline

My desire is not to write a how-to book for parents. However, when it comes to establishing forms of discipline that glorify God, it's essential to consider the state of our hearts and minds when discipline needs to happen.

To do this, let's consider the heart and mind of our heavenly Father towards us when we need discipline.

But God demonstrates His own love toward us, in that while we were yet sinners, Christ died for us.
Romans 5:8

Jesus Christ only did what he saw his Father do. While the work was missional, the reason was relational. All of us have sinned. We teased our younger siblings or talked rudely to the school bus driver. We shunned the new kid at school or prostituted ourselves with an ungodly lifestyle. Jesus revealed His lovingkindness by paying the cost for our misdeeds. That's how much He cares about His relationship with us. He does not send us to our rooms, but He says, "Son or Daughter, come to My lap and let Me love you into change." Wow. How beautiful and wonderful is the Savior of our souls! His mercy is new every morning!

As we discipline our children, we want to model the Father. It's helpful to first pray to God for His grace and mercy to reign in our hearts. Regularly, I have to remind myself not to rush discipline by announcing the consequence. The better way is to first go to our kids and say, "I love you in spite of what you have done." Then boundaries and disciplinary measures can be assigned and explained. It's not easy. When two kids are yelling at each other, sometimes we do need to say, "You go sit here, and you go over there and calm down for a moment!" My point is that we must remember that we do not discipline to feel a sense of vengeance or to release anger. That would be unkind. We discipline to teach consequences and to protect.

Kindness means being considerate and warm-hearted. It is a platform of mercy. Our words and our hands are meant to reflect God. As we affirm and as we serve, we can build up those around us. Saying and showing "I love you" and "I am interested in you" to our kids regularly, cultivates emotional connection that can be disrupted when they do need discipline. Those words also help us to develop a healthy family culture.

How Kind Are We to Ourselves?

Once at a church prayer meeting, a pastor shared that God had him thinking about what people think about themselves. Their self-talk and self-concept. We can be so unkind to ourselves. Hopefully, as you've read through the book, you've learned that God is very patient with you. Maybe you've been able to take time and think about what grace really means and how it is shown to you daily. We are on a journey of becoming whole. Not only is it unfair, but it is unhealthy to entertain self-condemnation, shame, guilt, and so many other life-stealing thoughts.

What words come to your mind when you think of yourself? The way we think of ourselves and treat ourselves often breaks the Father's heart. He who took our sin and our sorrow, because He loves us, wants us to love ourselves. We cannot fully love one another until we love ourselves. But how do we love ourselves when we sometimes don't like ourselves?

First, it means we have to forgive ourselves. It's fine, even healthy, to feel bad for something we've done wrong or an attitude that we'd adopted, but as we experience remorse, we must remember that God is full of mercy, compassion, and help. Maybe you don't like your personality or what you look like. You've probably compared yourself with someone else, who has qualities that you have subconsciously elevated. The truth is, each of us has distinctions according to God's design and intent. While sin, inherited weaknesses, and our environment can cause distortions to His design for us, God, our Potter is continuously working on us—mending and cultivating our souls. As far as feeling bad for what we've done wrong, despite natural consequences that we may have to deal with, our identity—the words that we use to describe ourselves—must be in alignment with the work of the Cross. Our identity can never be based on our behavior or feelings.

We need to let God be our Judge, not ourselves. The amazing fact is that as our Judge, once we, as believers, acknowledge our sin, our mistakes, and our hurts, they are automatically assigned to Jesus Christ. We are released.

My favorite Bible verse is Jeremiah 31:3. It makes my heart glad. Here are a few verses from this chapter that reveal that God has endless vision and hope for you and me. We are His children and while He sees our present state, He knows our end.

The Lord appeared to him from afar, saying,
"I have loved you with an everlasting love;
therefore I have drawn you with lovingkindness.
Again I will build you and you will be rebuilt,
O virgin of Israel!
Again you will take up your tambourines,
and go forth to the dances of the merrymakers.
Again you will plant vineyards
on the hills of Samaria;
the planters will plant and will enjoy them."
Jeremiah 31:2-5

This passage is rich with God's intent for good in spite of Israel's imperfections. Being kind to ourselves means receiving His lovingkindness. This can be hard when we feel so unworthy. The truth is, we are unworthy. But He's kind anyway and in this realization, we can rejoice. He is love.

I encourage you to think back through your life and remember any demeaning names or negative phrases that you were called, or people's opinions of you that stuck to you. These need to be brought to the Cross. Jesus looked out among the crowd and cried to God, "Father, forgive them, for they know not what they do." Often people don't understand the power of their words, the not-so-funny nicknames, or casual remarks that wound our self-concept. Ask the Holy Spirit to help you forgive these people and even forgive you if you've called yourself something that Jesus never would.

Lovingkindness centers on the Cross. This is the place where the vertical relationship between us and God, and the horizontal relationships between each us meet at the intersection of Jesus' sacrifice. He showed His love for us so that we can love ourselves and therefore love one another. This was a kind act. One that put the other—us, before Himself. Jesus pushed through the pain, to gain the prize set before Him, which was us.

We will have to do this repeatedly as parents, that is, extend kindness despite how we feel. Our kids will say things out of brokenness or immaturity that will hurt us. And we will do the same for them. Lovingkindness can be hard and inconvenient, but it blesses someone else and it repels the evil one. The devil wants to destroy our relationships. Division is an evil tactic. But walking in lovingness protects our relationships and matures us as people of God.

Prayer

Great and gracious Father, sometimes it's hard to find the words to express my gratitude for what You do for me. The words, "Thank You" seems insufficient. When I push pause on my daily agenda and take the time to consider Your kindness, I'm undone. I'm humbled. I'm eternally grateful. God, You are so wonderful. You are so other-focused. Help me and my family to be like this. Help us be kind when it hurts. When we experience a deep wound or transgression against us, help us know that You were with us the very moment we got hurt. Tend to every subconscious memory and part of us that still retains sorrow and trauma from the incident. Help us process old hurts with You and find refuge in You. In Jesus' name, Amen.

Quiet Time

Write down or think about how God has shown you kindness.

Recollect how you felt when someone did something kind for you.

Ask God to heal any part of you that struggles to be kind because of a deep wound or traumatic event. The Holy Spirit may bring forgiveness to your mind. Forgiveness doesn't instantly remove the hurt—the emotional pain. It's a decision of the will to release the person from their offense.

Chapter Eleven

Embracing His Likeness

But the fruit of the Spirit is love, joy, peace, patience, kindness, goodness, faithfulness, gentleness, self-control.
Galatians 5:22

In the public library one day, I found a parenting article in a magazine that was quite eye-opening. Was I the classic helicopter parent, or was I too lenient and lax? I found these questions condescending. As a woman that dislikes labels and stereotypes, I concluded that these parent labels must have been coined by experts who don't realize that there are times when parents need to be helicopters and times when we need to be lenient. Sure, perhaps our individual personalities carry a particular bent, but if we learn how to parent according to Scripture, then we will realize that parenting is less about the degree in which we orchestrate the details of our children's lives and more about how well we allow a wise and adoring God to parent our kids through us. I gained this perspective at a parenting workshop

Was I the classic helicopter parent, or was I too lenient and lax?

years ago. I heard someone say, "They are His kids, We are the stewards."

Our view of God is crucial. If we disregard His divine authority, then instead of being submitted stewards, we'll function like an autocrat—domineering and repressive.

God's Parenting Style

As kids, many of us were introduced to a stern God. An all-knowing being that would strike us down if we ever used His name in vain. His holiness made us nervous as we walked into the church sanctuary thinking *"Will He tell the pastor what I did yesterday?"* Because of the way we thought of God, communing with Him was mostly an act of religious practice—reciting phrases from prayer books, taking communion, and fear-laden silence. We were timid in the presence of the God of the Old Testament, who killed His enemies with no remorse. But look at this passage:

The LORD your God in your midst,
The Mighty One, will save; He will rejoice over you with gladness,
He will quiet you with His love,
He will rejoice over you with singing.
Zephaniah 3: 17

And then we read John 14:9 which says, *He who has seen Me, has seen the Father; how can you say 'Show us the Father'? Do you not believe that I am in the Father, and the Father is in Me?"* We scratch our heads because Jesus is far too kind and friendly—even letting a disciple lay back on His chest, to be like the Father. Passages like this reveal a different version of God, or I'd say a deeper revelation of God than we were first taught. *His anger is but for a moment, but His favor is for a lifetime* (Psalm 30:5). This is the revelation that David had of God. David, the one who killed a man and then slept with his wife, tells us in many verses that God's anger doesn't last long. In fact, He doesn't get angry with us quickly. Furthermore, Psalm 86:15 says that His favor, compassion, and mercy are abounding! Is this your view of God? If you've ever had difficulty relating to Him in the same way you relate to Jesus, could this be the reason why?

The truth is, the way we raise our kids will reflect how we relate to God's fatherly heart. We are made to be image-bearers and we will be. The problem is: whose image are we bearing—the Father that Jesus spent time with on the mountain, or an image skewed by a faulty human lens. Or perhaps your earthly dad made such an impression on you, that you are bearing his image...but it doesn't reflect God, the Father. Jesus has defined the Father for us. When Jesus was baptized, the Father called down, "That's my Son! He hasn't done any miracle yet or laid down His life yet, but I'm pleased with Him!" As a child of God, do you know that you give Him pleasure? Not because of what you do or don't do. But because you belong to Him. Our perspective of the parental nature of God is integral to our health and wholeness. We can't possibly run to a heavenly Father who we think is always criticizing us, watching us with a stern eye or ready to take some of His blessings back for our bad behavior. Similarly, our kids won't run to us if we are always critical, stern, or conditional with our love and acceptance.

We can't possibly run to a heavenly Father who we think is always criticizing us.

God desires our best. He is the perfect Parent. He works through the avenues of our lives and breaks up the fallow ground of our hearts (Hosea 10:12) to bring forth our best. Sometimes His working can be more subtle or slower than we prefer. But let us remember that not only does He coach us but He sits on the sidelines cheering us on. When we struggle or are weak and ask

Him for help, He mercifully and graciously steps into the game and helps us reach the end zone. Sometimes the end zone isn't the idyllic conclusion that we want, but it will be a place where we are more mature.

Love Fight For Our Success

We have to remember that life has real opponents, spiritual and natural. The demonic realm seeks to destroy us, and issues like sickness, finances, and family divisiveness can stress us. The fact is this: through Jesus, every parent can end well. At the end of our earthly life, He'll say, "Well done, my good and faithful servant." Victory is the theme of the last chapter of your journey and mine. Romans 2:4 says that the kindness of God leads us to repentance. Repentance is having a change of mindset. How ironic that by continuing to unleash His kindness towards us, we will slowly but surely change the way we think for the better. As our thinking changes, we make different decisions. We prioritize and hold on to what is most valuable to God. We grow as we go—moving forward despite any momentary setbacks. The seasons of life continue, and we learn that the symbolism of Ecclesiastes 3:5-7 is true for all of us.

A time to cast away stones, (DEMOLISH)
And a time to gather stones; (BUILDING)
A time to embrace, (JOINING)
And a time to refrain from embracing; (LIMITING)
A time to gain, (RECEIVING)
And a time to lose; (LAY ASIDE)
A time to keep, (TREASURING)
And a time to throw away; (FORSAKING)
A time to tear, (CONSECRATING)
And a time to sew; (HEALING)

I used to read this passage and think that these "times" were out of my control. But now I see that decision-making is a subtle theme throughout these verses. Whether it's the decision to tear myself away from my usual distractions to spend time with God or whether I need to reach out to someone that hurt me, I have to determine God's route to wholeness. Maybe some of you are in a season where you have to set some limits for yourself. Or lay aside goals to make more time for your kids. Perhaps this is a time of receiving God's help and direction so that you can be freed from bitterness or anxiety that is affecting your physical health.

Maybe some of you are in a season where you have to set some limits for yourself.

This passage does apply to God's oversight of our lives, too. Because He wants what is best for us, the Father gives us insight and wisdom on how to live. God of the Bible is not a distant god who leaves us to figure this journey out on our own. He is love. And love goes out of its way for the good of "the loved". We are "the loved" and He teaches us how to remove obstacles that keep us from receiving the fullness—the abundance of His love. Not only does He do this for us, but He does this for our kids.

The Push and Pull of Love

One Saturday morning, instead of running into your arms, your young daughter runs onto the couch to watch her morning cartoon. You shrug your shoulders and get her breakfast. The next week the same thing happens. You notice a decrease in the number of times that she crawls onto your lap or lays her head on your shoulder or turns to wave before heading into the school building. This shift may happen all at once or over the years.

But at first, it catches you off guard. Then you slowly begin to mourn the inevitable ending of a stage. Over time, you get used to the new norm. As she gets older, you hope that the security you instilled during those intimate snuggle times on the couch was consistent enough to stay in her memory banks as she journeys through adolescence.

As parents, it's instinctual to begin to push our young ones away incrementally. At first, it may be weaning the baby from the breast. Next, it may be teaching them how to put on their clothes by themselves. Our kids sometimes give us the queues when they are ready for another level of autonomy. For some dads, signs of a new stage might be when your kids want to hang out with friends instead of going fishing or watching sports with you. Their total dependence on us must end at some point. As stewards, we have to know when and how to nudge them outward—lessening their dependence upon us. These opportunities can be anything from being left alone at home to running into the grocery store for you.

At the same time, we don't want to short circuit their natural need for parental covering. Sense of identity and security begins at home in the formative years and continues through adolescence. Some people believe that quality time is better than quantity time. I don't think this way. It depends on the child. I've surprisingly found that some of our teens enjoyed quantity time as much as quality time. This push into healthy autonomy and security must occur at various points and is based on an individual child's developmental timetable. The push is normal.

Sense of identity and security begins at home in the formative years and continues through adolescence.

However, sometimes when we see how well our kids are adapting, we realize that we miss them needing us—them reaching for us. The morning snuggle. Throwing the baseball around outside. We looked forward to "the embrace" before heading out the door to work and we are tempted to pull these precious God-breathed souls back into us to smell their hair or to find comfort in them still needing our presence. This type of pull is understandable, but it can be a sign of codependency. Our wellbeing can not be dependant upon the presence of our kids. When it is, the relationship gets messy.

What is a healthy pull? Let's study our heavenly Father. He keeps His arms wide open and draws us into His sheltering presence (Psalm 91). He delights when we come to Him. He enjoys it when we want to know more about Him (James 2:23). He comes to find us when we are hiding (Genesis 3:9). He looks expectantly for us when we've gone astray (Luke 15:11-32). His shepherding does not end when we reach a certain age. This pull is powerfully precious. We need it. At the same time, our Heavenly Father tells us to go—go out and represent Him in all that we do and say, especially to those people that have not yet recognized His reality (Mark 16:15). At some point, He wants us to let go of the childish stage of our faith journey and step into a mature partnership with Him (1 Cor. 13:11).

We are created to be image-bearers who reflect not the world's ways, but our heavenly Father's ways. We'll push our children when it is time for them to grow into another stage yet "pull" them toward us to continually remind them that we adore them, that we will be safe for them and that we will always have open arms for them. The push is not to their detriment, and it is not based on our convenience. The pull should neither serve our own needs nor stifle their individuality. Instead, both the push and the pull maintain the security of a healthy relationship and the value of growing up.

Let's turn the tables on ourselves. Earlier, I talked about how the way we view God will determine how we relate to Him. How often do we crawl into our coziest chair and gleefully open our Bibles to discover something that God wants to share with us? How often do we let ourselves realize how much He adores us! God pulls us into His presence to give us security. He's always there. He never forsakes us. He pushes us out, but only so that we can give what He's poured into us. It's a back and forth game that a child would play with a parent. Maybe you've witnessed a scene like this, the cute giggles as a little girl runs to her daddy's lap, and then runs several feet away for a few seconds only to run back to her daddy's loving embrace.

Your Spring is Here

Maybe while reading this book, you have discovered an area that God wants to work on in your life or your family life. I began with the analogy of digging. Looking under the surface of souls to find root systems related to past hurts, inherited weaknesses or incorrect mindsets. This process must be Spirit-led for only God can reveal seeds that bring forth habits, motives, and responses that hinder our maturity. He demolishes weed structures to grow healthy root systems that will stand the test of time. I encourage you to journal or find a friend or counselor to talk with about different things that you've realized by reading this book. Also, if you are married, consider reading this book with your spouse. Being on the same page is always helpful.

Child-rearing bears fruit, although the ripening takes years to happen. As we raise our kids, we must remain open to the necessary pruning and grafting that this journey brings. A humble parent who lives yielded to the molding hand of God will do more to assist their children's development than any lecture, form of discipline, or parenting book. We must be patient. Each virtue in the fruit of the Spirit will become more apparent as we spend time with God in prayer and reflection.

God is rebuilding families right now. At the end of our church service, we have a time of altar prayer. Sometimes when I serve in this way and pray for people, the request is for God to help with family conflict. After praying for the individual, sometimes I'm impressed to share with them that their courage and action to come for prayer opens the door for family restoration. I share about the mission that Moses had. Moses heard God's call to lead his people out of Egypt, which is a symbol of bondage. God often delivers an individual first and then allows that individual to partner with Him to restore a whole family, even generations of a family line.

I end this book with a passage from the Song of Solomon. This Old Testament book metaphorically links marital love with the love of Christ for His Bride: those who have received Him as Lord and Savior. This passage is an encouragement for you to arise. Your "spring" is here. The fruit of the Spirit is coming forth in your life. Jesus, our Divine Shepherd, will lead you in your journey of soul health. "Arise, my darling, my beautiful one, and come along."

Arise, my darling, my beautiful one, And come along.
For behold, the winter is past, The rain is over and gone.
The flowers have already appeared in the land;
The time has arrived for pruning the vines,
And the voice of the turtledove has been heard in our land.
The fig tree has ripened its figs,
And the vines in blossom have given forth their fragrance.
Arise, my darling, my beautiful one, And come along!
Song of Solomon 2: 10-13

My Prayer for You

Lord, I thank you for everyone who has read this book. Bless them. Continue to lead them toward wholeness. As they spend time with You and in the fellowship of spiritually healthy believers, cultivate the soil of their souls. Help them avoid self-condemnation and guilt as they become more self-aware. Teach them how to relate to You as a Parent so that You can help them raise emotionally healthy children. Tear away wrong perceptions of You. Convince them that You are for them and not against them. Jesus, You said, "And I will send you the Divine Encourager from the very presence of my Father. He will come to you, the spirit of Truth, emanating from the Father, and he will speak to you about me."(John 15: 26 TPT) I pray each mother and father would sense the encouragement of the Holy Spirit and be empowered by Him, their Comforter, their Guide, and their Advocate. In Jesus' name. Amen

Quiet Time

Which chapters impacted you the most?

Why did they impact you?

Spend time in praise and thanksgiving. Thank Him for what He has highlighted and what He has healed.

Consider sharing with someone what you gained through reading this book. Our testimony is a gateway through which God is glorified and others gain hope.

Cultivating BOOKSeries

"Growing in Him to Love One Another"

tinawebb.net

Future Titles

Cultivating our Family Ties - Pursuing Spiritual and Emotional Growth Together

Cultivating the Souls of Children – Godly Soil, God's Seeds, God's Growth

About the Author

Tina Webb is a lay minister and life coach for people wanting to engage God for emotional well-being. She and her husband have six children, and she was a home educator for twenty years. In 2020 she became a Certified Apprentice Facilitator in Classic Trauma Healing through the Trauma Healing Institute.

Podcast:

Digging Deep – Life Talk with Doug and Tina/
The 14- Minute Momlife Pause

Books:

Culture Changers – Understand the Roots of Brokenness and Help Heal Your Family and Community

Justice Reframed – How the Cross Confronts Our Pursuit of Justice

Visit tinawebb.net to subscribe to Tina's newsletter.
Website: tinawebb.net **Instagram:** tina.w.webb **Twitter:** @WebbBegin

Consider writing a review on an online site like Amazon so that other parents and guardians can discover this resource.